The HUGE Book of Amazing Facts & Interesting Stuff

Christmas Edition

BELLANOVA

MELBOURNE · SOFIA · BERLIN

The HUGE Book of Amazing Facts and Interesting Stuff: Christmas Edition

www.bellanovabooks.com

Contents

Introduction

Welcome to The HUGE Book of Amazing Facts and Interesting Stuff: Christmas Edition!

Ho, ho, ho! We're excited to introduce our inaugural Christmas Edition, and we've made our list (and checked it twice) to ensure that this version is festive, fun, and filled with facts fit for the season.

Much has transpired since our last edition, including the events in Europe and the steps we've taken towards a semblance of normalcy in 2022 after two whirlwind years. As we embrace the festive spirit and bid farewell to another year, it's the perfect time to delve into Christmas-themed trivia and tales.

From the mysterious origins of age-old traditions to wacky world records surrounding the festive period, this edition is a hearty mix of yuletide yarns and winter wonders. Whether you're seeking stories to share around the fireplace or looking to learn more about the most wonderful time of the year, this edition has got you covered.

So, throw on your favorite Christmas sweater, brew a cup of cocoa, and dive into a world of merry mysteries and jolly jests. Enjoy, and may your days be merry and bright!

The History of Christmas

Deck the halls and journey back in time! Christmas, the jolliest holiday of them all, boasts traditions, stories, and customs that span centuries and continents. But how did it all begin? How did a mid-winter festival evolve into the modern extravaganza of twinkling lights, carol singing, and gift exchanges? From ancient pagan practices to Victorian-era festivities, we're about to unwrap the rich tapestry of Christmas's past.

So, stoke the fire and settle in as we recount the festive tales of yesteryears.

The term "Christmas" derives from the Old English phrase "Cristes Maesse," which means "Christ's Mass." Over time, "Cristes Maesse" evolved into the modern English term "Christmas." Or was it to save ink on Christmas cards? We'll never know.

🦌 🦌 🦌

Jesus was born on December 25th—allegedly. The Bible never specified a date. Despite the absence of a divine birth certificate, the date stuck.

🦌 🦌 🦌

Early Christians didn't originally celebrate Jesus' birth, but as the faith spread in Rome, they began to commemorate it during the same time as Saturnalia, Rome's winter fest known for gift-giving and parties. And the Romans sure knew how to throw a toga party!

Sol Invictus, another Roman festival, also fell on December 25th. Because why have one party when you can have two?

🦌 🦌 🦌

The year 336 AD saw the first "official" Christmas, thanks to Emperor Constantine. He made it cool to celebrate.

🦌 🦌 🦌

Emperor Constantine also made Christianity the "it" religion in Rome. In 313 AD, he issued the Edict of Milan, which granted religious tolerance to Christians. He did not, however, make Christianity the official religion of the Roman Empire; that honor goes to Emperor Theodosius I in 380 AD. Move over, paganism!

The U.S. was fashionably late to the Christmas party, only making it a federal holiday in 1870.

🦌 🦌 🦌

"Silent Night" had its world premiere in 1818 in Austria. Now, it's the soundtrack to awkward family dinners worldwide.

🦌 🦌 🦌

The first-ever Christmas card was created in 1843. It's been downhill since, with e-cards and GIFs taking over.

🦌 🦌 🦌

The Puritans banned Christmas from 1659 to 1681. Somebody needed to lighten up, huh?

Post-Revolution Russia gave Christmas the cold shoulder until 1992. Although it wasn't officially banned, public celebrations were frowned upon. That's a long time without tinsel.

⁂

The Twelve Days of Christmas: not just a catchy song but a legit season. The "Twelve Days of Christmas" represents the time between Christmas Day and the Epiphany (January 6th) in many Christian traditions. No word on whether the five golden rings are 24 karat, though.

⁂

A boar's head was the Christmas meal of choice in Medieval England. At least they didn't have to worry about overcooking a turkey.

Before beards and hipster vibes were cool, 'Sinterklaas,' the OG Dutch Santa, was rocking the look. Influencing our modern Santa Claus, he was the trendsetter you probably didn't know about! Americans morphed "Sinterklaas" into "Santa Claus." New country, new brand.

🦌 🦌 🦌

Germans started the indoor Christmas tree trend in the 16th century. You can thank them for pine needles in your living room.

🦌 🦌 🦌

Legend has it that Martin Luther was the first to bling out a Christmas tree with candles. Inspired by a starry night or just setting 16th-century trends? Either way, someone pass the fire extinguisher!

Oliver Cromwell tried to hit the "mute" button on Christmas in 1647. Spoiler: England wasn't having it. King Charles II hit "unmute" on Christmas in England in 1660. Queue the festive comeback!

🦌 🦌 🦌

In early America, Christmas was the underdog holiday. Easter had all the glory.

🦌 🦌 🦌

The Christmas Truce of 1914 saw soldiers from opposing sides playing soccer and sharing food. Turns out, holiday cheer is contagious, even in trenches.

Irving Berlin, who penned "White Christmas," was Jewish. He wrote a Christmas classic but never had to fuss with tinsel or mistletoe.

🦌 🦌 🦌

The Russian Orthodox Church celebrates Christmas on January 7 due to the use of the Julian calendar.

🦌 🦌 🦌

Franklin Pierce, 14th President of the U.S., was the first to put up an official White House Christmas tree in 1856. Imagine being the Secret Service agents tasked with ornament duty.

Coca-Cola popularized the modern image of Santa Claus in the 1930s, dressing him in their corporate colors. Best marketing gig ever?

🦌 🦌 🦌

In 1882, Edward Johnson, a colleague of Thomas Edison, was the first to string electric lights on a Christmas tree. Edison: "Why didn't I think of that?"

🦌 🦌 🦌

Washington Irving, author of "Sleepy Hollow," penned "The Sketch Book of Geoffrey Crayon, Gent." which popularized Christmas traditions in America.

In 350 AD, it is believed Pope Julius I declared December 25 as the official date of Christmas. Because when the Pope sets a calendar invite, you don't decline.

🦌 🦌 🦌

Kwanzaa, established in 1966, sometimes coincides with Christmas but serves to celebrate African heritage. It's like the new kid on the holiday block.

🦌 🦌 🦌

The 1968 Christmas Eve space broadcast had astronauts reading from the Book of Genesis. Nothing says Christmas like a holiday greeting from space!

"O Holy Night" was the second piece of music ever broadcast on radio in 1906. Before Spotify, that was peak tech!

🦌 🦌 🦌

The iconic red suit of Santa Claus was popularized by Thomas Nast, a 19th-century political cartoonist. Who says fashion can't be political?

🦌 🦌 🦌

In 1912, New York City's first public Christmas tree lit up Madison Square Park. At 60 feet tall, it was basically the skyscraper of trees!

Advent, the period of preparation for Christmas, starts on November 30 or December 1, depending on the calendar you follow. As if you needed an excuse to start celebrating early.

🦌 🦌 🦌

Some believe the tradition of hanging stockings comes from a Dutch legend involving St. Nicholas and three impoverished sisters. The original Cinderella story, but with less glass—more wooly socks.

Eggnog has its roots in medieval Europe, inspired by various creamy alcoholic beverages, including the English "posset." Fast forward, and today's "eggnog" might be easier on the tongue, especially after a glass or two.

🦌 🦌 🦌

In Mexico, Christmas is celebrated from December 12 to January 6. Talk about a marathon, not a sprint.

🦌 🦌 🦌

The most expensively decorated Christmas tree was worth around $11 million and was displayed in Marbella, Spain, in 2018. It was probably too precious to put presents under.

The concept of "boxing" up goods for the poor led to the creation of Boxing Day on December 26. It's like the afterparty for do-gooders.

🦌 🦌 🦌

German settlers in Pennsylvania set up the first recorded instance of a Christmas tree in the United States in 1816. The pioneers were also the first to introduce holiday decor.

🦌 🦌 🦌

The poinsettia plant, native to Mexico, is named after Joel Roberts Poinsett, the first U.S. Minister to Mexico, who introduced it in America in the 1820s. How do you say "Merry Christmas" in botanical?

Norway gifts London with a Christmas tree each year as a thank-you for British support during WWII. Nothing says "thank you" like a 20-meter spruce!

🦌 🦌 🦌

The tradition of Christmas markets dates back to the Late Middle Ages in German-speaking Europe. Talk about a centuries-old shopping spree.

🦌 🦌 🦌

The first Salvation Army Christmas kettle appeared in San Francisco in 1891 to feed the needy.

The first evidence of a Christmas feast dates back to 1213, orchestrated by King John of England. The menu? Wine and mutton, of course!

🦌 🦌 🦌

According to data from 2015, Christmas is responsible for nearly 30% of annual jewelry sales. That's a lot of sparkly Christmas mornings!

🦌 🦌 🦌

In Japan, eating KFC on Christmas Eve is a beloved tradition, thanks to a successful marketing campaign in the 1970s. Finger-lickin' festive, wouldn't you say?

The largest-ever gathering of Santa Clauses involved 18,112 participants and took place in Kerala, India, in 2014. SantaCon, eat your heart out.

🦌 🦌 🦌

The candy cane is believed to date back to 1670 in Germany and was created to keep children quiet in church. An ancient "mute" button, if you will.

🦌 🦌 🦌

The longest-running Christmas TV special is "Rudolph the Red-Nosed Reindeer," first airing in 1964. Never underestimate the staying power of a reindeer with a glowing nose.

The Nutcracker ballet premiered in St. Petersburg, Russia, in 1892 and was initially deemed a failure. But now, it pirouettes into our hearts every holiday season.

🦌 🦌 🦌

According to Guinness World Records, the tallest cut Christmas tree was a 221-foot Douglas fir displayed in 1950 at the Northgate Shopping Center in Seattle. You'd need a ladder for those top ornaments!

🦌 🦌 🦌

The custom of kissing under mistletoe comes from ancient Norse mythology. Even the gods needed a little help with their love lives.

The first known use of the word "eggnog" was in 1775. It's unclear when the first eggnog hangover was recorded.

❄ ❄ ❄

The world's largest Christmas stocking, according to Guinness World Records, was 168 feet long and 70 feet wide, created in Tuscany, Italy in 2011. Imagine the size of the fireplace!

❄ ❄ ❄

"All I Want for Christmas Is You" by Mariah Carey finally hit #1 on the Billboard Hot 100 chart 25 years after its release in 2019. A slow burn, but a hot one.

In the Philippines, the Christmas season starts
in September and ends in January. They win the
award for longest holiday season!

🦌 🦌 🦌

According to Statistics Canada, 3.5 million fruitcakes
are sold annually in the country. Whether they are
eaten or not remains a mystery.

🦌 🦌 🦌

In 1965, astronauts aboard the Gemini 6 spacecraft
played "Jingle Bells" on a harmonica and bells,
marking the first musical performance in space.
Houston, we have a carol.

Each year, roughly 33 million real Christmas trees are sold in the United States. That's a lot of pine-scented air fresheners.

🦌 🦌 🦌

During WWII, for a unique Christmas gift, the U.S. Playing Card Company crafted decks for POWs that, when soaked, showed escape maps out of Germany. What's better than the gift of freedom for the holidays?

"Christmas." 2023. Encyclopædia Britannica. Encyclopædia Britannica, inc. September 26. https://www.britannica.com/topic/Christmas.

"Saturnalia: Meaning, Festival & Christmas - HISTORY." 2023. History.Com. A&E Television Networks. Accessed September 27. https://www.history.com/topics/ancient-rome/saturnalia.

"Why Is Christmas in December?" 2023. Encyclopædia Britannica. Encyclopædia Britannica, inc. Accessed September 27. https://www.britannica.com/story/why-is-christmas-in-december

Waxman, Olivia B. 2016. "Christmas: Surprising Story of the Holiday in America." Time. Time. December 23. https://time.com/4608452/christmas-america-national-holiday/.

"Silent Night." 2023. Wikipedia. Wikimedia Foundation. September 21. https://en.wikipedia.org/wiki/Silent_Night.

"The First Christmas Card." 2023. The Postal Museum. https://www.postal-museum.org/collections/first-christmas-card.

"When Massachusetts Banned Christmas." 2023. History.Com. A&E Television Networks. Accessed September 27. https://www.history.com/news/when-massachusetts-banned-christmas.

"Christmas in Russia." 2023. Wikipedia. Wikimedia Foundation. September 24. https://en.wikipedia.org/wiki/Christmas_in_Russia.

"Boar's Head Festival." 2023. Concordia University Ann Arbor. Accessed September 27. https://www.cuaa.edu/life/kreft-arts/boars-head.html.

"Sinterklaas." 2023. Wikipedia. Wikimedia Foundation. September 24. https://en.wikipedia.org/wiki/Sinterklaas.

"History of Christmas Trees - Symbolism, Traditions & Trivia." 2023. History.Com. A&E Television Networks. Accessed September 27. https://www.history.com/topics/christmas/history-of-christmas-trees.

Foundation, Arbor Day. 2022. "History of the Christmas Tree." Arbor Day Blog. March 16. https://arbordayblog.org/holiday/history-of-the-christmas-tree/.

"Did Oliver Cromwell Really Ban Christmas?" 2023. Historic England. Accessed September 27. https://historicengland.org.uk/listing/what-is-designation/heritage-highlights/did-oliver-cromwell-really-ban-christmas/.

"The Three Kings: Why Spain Celebrates a Second Christmas with the Reyes Magos on January 6." 2023. ! ! Murcia Today - The Three Kings: Why Spain Celebrates A Second Christmas With The Reyes Magos On January 6. Accessed September 27. https://murciatoday.com/the_three_kings_why_spain_celebrates_a_second_christmas_with_the_reyes_magos_on_january_6_1962011-a.html.

Burton, Tara Isabella. 2018. "Why Easter Never Became a Big Secular Holiday like Christmas." Vox. March 29. https://www.vox.com/2018/3/29/17168804/why-easter-celebrate-big-secular-holiday-like-christmas-bunny-egg-pagan.

"The Success Story of Irving Berlin." 2023. Red Star Line Museum. Accessed September 27. https://redstarline.be/en/story/success-story-irving-berlin.

Cillizza, Chris. 2021. "You Can Thank Franklin Pierce for the White House Christmas Tree." The Washington Post. WP Company. November 25. https://www.washingtonpost.com/news/the-fix/wp/2016/11/10/you-can-thank-franklin-pierce-for-the-white-house-christmas-tree/.

"Who Invented Electric Christmas Lights?" 2023. The Library of Congress. Accessed September 27. https://www.loc.gov/everyday-mysteries/technology/item/who-invented-electric-christmas-lights/#:~:text=Edward%20H.,them%20around%20his%20Christmas%20tree.

"The Sketch Book." 2023. Encyclopædia Britannica. Encyclopædia Britannica, inc. Accessed September 27. https://www.britannica.com/topic/The-Sketch-Book.

The Editor: Italy On This Day. 1970. Pope Julius I. https://www.italyonthisday.com/2020/04/pope-julius-i-Christmas-December-25.html.

"Kwanzaa." 2023. Encyclopædia Britannica. Encyclopædia Britannica, inc. August 8. https://www.britannica.com/topic/Kwanzaa.

Jones, Meg. 2018. "50 Years Ago, Apollo 8 Astronauts Orbited the Moon and United a Troubled Earth." Journal Sentinel. Milwaukee Journal Sentinel. December 23. https://eu.jsonline.com/story/news/2018/12/21/50-years-ago-apollo-8-astronauts-saved-1968-genesis-reading/2301420002/.

Ambrosino, Brandon. 2014. "The X in Xmas Literally Means Christ. Here's the History behind It." Vox. Vox. December 14. https://www.vox.com/2014/12/14/7374401/jesus-xmas-christmas.

Fung, Brian. 2021. "Merry Christmas! 107 Years Ago Tonight, Americans Heard the World's First Radio Show." The Washington Post. WP Company. December 6. https://www.washingtonpost.com/news/the-switch/wp/2013/12/24/merry-christmas-107-years-ago-tonight-americans-heard-the-worlds-first-ever-radio-show/.

Magazine, Smithsonian. 2018. "A Civil War Cartoonist Created the Modern Image of Santa Claus as Union Propaganda." Smithsonian.Com. Smithsonian Institution. December 19. https://www.smithsonianmag.com/history/civil-war-cartoonist-created-modern-image-santa-claus-union-propaganda-180971074/.

"Holiday Tree." 2021. Madison Square Park Conservancy. April 2. https://madisonsquarepark.org/community/news/2021/04/holiday-tree/.

Sockshop. 2023. "The Legend of Christmas Stockings." The Legend of Christmas Stockings | The SockShop Blog. Accessed September 27. https://www.sockshop.co.uk/blog/posts/december-2015/the-legend-of-christmas-stockings.

Pupovac, Jessica. 2013. "Writing 'Rudolph': The Original Red-Nosed Manuscript." NPR. NPR. December 25. https://www.npr.org/2013/12/25/256579598/writing-rudolph-the-original-red-nosed-manuscript.

"Red Crab Migration." 2023. Australian Government. Accessed September 27. https://parksaustralia.gov.au/christmas/discover/highlights/red-crab-migration/.

Knight, Rebecca. 2019. "Is This the Most Expensive Christmas Tree in the World? It Cost £12 Million and Is Dripping in Diamonds." Ideal Home. Ideal Home. December 9. https://www.idealhome.co.uk/news/most-expensive-christmas-tree-239460.

"Ethiopian Christmas." 2023. Wikipedia. Wikimedia Foundation. April 30. https://en.wikipedia.org/wiki/Ethiopian_Christmas.

"Boxing Day." 2023. Wikipedia. Wikimedia Foundation. September 14.

https://en.wikipedia.org/wiki/Boxing_Day.
"Extension Educationin Bexar County." 2023. Urban Program Bexar County. Accessed September 27. https://bexar-tx.tamu.edu/homehort/archives-of-weekly-articles-davids-plant-of-the-week/a-little-bit-of-history-about-christmas-trees.

"Joel Roberts Poinsett." 2023. Wikipedia. Wikimedia Foundation. March 3. https://es.wikipedia.org/wiki/Joel_Roberts_Poinsett.

"The Trafalgar Square Christmas Tree Is a Gift from Norway." 2023. Visit Norway. Accessed September 27. https://www.visitnorway.com/typically-norwegian/christmas/the-trafalgar-square-christmas-tree/.

Magazine, Smithsonian. 2022. "A Brief History of Christmas Markets." Smithsonian.Com. Smithsonian Institution. December 19. https://www.smithsonianmag.com/history/a-brief-history-of-christmas-markets-180981308.

"Krampus." 2023. Encyclopædia Britannica. Encyclopædia Britannica, inc. September 8. https://www.britannica.com/topic/Krampus.

"Red Kettles: The Salvation Army USA." 2023. Red Kettles | The Salvation Army USA. Accessed September 27. https://www.salvationarmyusa.org/usn/red-kettle-history/.

Alhays. 2019. The Trident. November 12. https://sites.owu.edu/trident/2017/11/04/holiday-traditions-in-the-middle-ages-by-christopher-shanley/.

Springer, Kate. 2022. "How KFC Became a Christmas Tradition in Japan." CNN. Cable News Network. December 22. https://edition.cnn.com/travel/article/kfc-christmas-tradition-japan/index.html.

Service, Indo-Asian News. 2014. "18,112 Santa Clauses Set Guinness Record in Kerala." NDTV.Com. December 27. https://www.ndtv.com/south/18-112-santa-clauses-set-guinness-record-in-kerala-7189530.

"Who Invented Candy Canes?" 2023. History.Com. A&E Television Networks. Accessed September 27. https://www.history.com/news/candy-canes-invented-germany.

"Rudolph the Red-Nosed Reindeer (TV Special)." 2023. Wikipedia. Wikimedia Foundation. September 11. https://en.wikipedia.org/wiki/Rudolph_the_Red-Nosed_Reindeer_(TV_special).

"Charles Dickens Partied HARD after Finishing A Christmas Carol in Just Six Weeks." 2022. Literary Hub. December 19. https://lithub.com/charles-dickens-partied-hard-after-finishing-a-christmas-carol-in-just-six-weeks/.

"The Nutcracker." 2023. Encyclopædia Britannica. Encyclopædia Britannica, inc. August 9. https://www.britannica.com/topic/The-Nutcracker.

"Tallest Christmas Tree." 2023. Guinness World Records. Accessed September 27. https://www.guinnessworldrecords.com/world-records/77271-tallest-christmas-tree.

Moon, Kat. 2018. "Why We Kiss Under the Mistletoe During Christmas." Time. Time. December 13. https://time.com/5471873/mistletoe-kiss-christmas/.

"Why Is It Called Eggnog? There's Some History Behind the Term." 2023. YourDictionary. YOURDICTIONARY. Accessed September 27. https://www.yourdictionary.com/articles/eggnog-history.

"Largest Christmas Stocking." 2023. Guinness World Records. Accessed September 27. https://www.guinnessworldrecords.com/world-records/largest-christmas-stocking.

Simons, Jordan. 2023. "The Philippines Starts Christmas in September." Travel Continuously. August 8. https://travelcontinuously.com/the-philippines-starts-christmas-in-september.

Brown, Dalvin. 2018. "Real vs. Fake Christmas Trees: Here's Why Some Americans Are Shifting Their Buying Habits." USA Today. Gannett Satellite Information Network. December 18. https://eu.usatoday.com/story/news/2018/12/14/real-vs-fake-heres-why-artificial-christmas-trees-rise/2314418002/.

"Stacking the Deck: Escape Cards of World War II (U.S. National Park Service)." 2023. National Parks Service. U.S. Department of the Interior. Accessed September 27. https://www.nps.gov/articles/000/stacking-the-deck-escape-cards-of-world-war-ii.htm.

Christmas Around the World

Pack your bags and put on your Santa hat, because we're embarking on a festive globe-trotting adventure! Christmas, while universally celebrated, is wonderfully diverse in its expressions. From the sun-soaked barbecues in Australia to the candlelit parades in Scandinavia, every corner of our world offers a unique spin on this beloved holiday. How do people in Iceland keep the chilly season bright?

In this chapter, we'll journey to various continents, unearthing the distinct customs, delicious foods, and delightful carols that make Christmas special to so many cultures. It's a reminder that while our traditions might differ, the spirit of joy and togetherness is universal. Ready to jet-set?

In Germany, children leave a shoe outside their house on December 5th, St. Nicholas' Day. If they've been good, they wake up to find it filled with treats. If they've been bad... well, let's not go there.

🎄🎄🎄

Venezuelans attend a daily early morning church service between December 16 and 24, known as "Misa de Aguinaldo."

🎄🎄🎄

In the Czech Republic, unmarried women toss a shoe over their shoulder on Christmas Eve for a festive spin on their love life forecast. If the shoe points to the door, it's time to shop for a wedding dress... and maybe new shoes!

Ukrainians decorate their Christmas trees with fake spider webs. It's based on a folktale where a spider spins a web around a poor family's tree, turning it silver and gold. So, move over, tinsel!

🎄🎄🎄

In Ethiopia, a game called "yeferas guks" is played at Christmas, which involves horse riders competing with one another. It's like the Kentucky Derby with a side of frankincense.

🎄🎄🎄

Greenland's Christmas cuisine includes "kiviak," a dish made by fermenting birds in sealskin. It's definitely not for the faint-hearted—or vegetarians.

🎄🎄🎄

Portugal's Christmas feast includes "consoda," a meal where extra places are set for deceased family members. It's spooky, but also heartwarming.

In Sweden, a giant straw goat called the "Gävle Goat" is erected in town squares. It often falls victim to arson, despite attempts to safeguard it. Apparently, some traditions are just too hot to handle.

🎄🎄🎄

In Italy, rather than Santa, the good witch "La Befana" delivers presents to children. Because why should old bearded men have all the fun?

🎄🎄🎄

Finland's Santa Claus, or "Joulupukki," traditionally lives in the Finnish Lapland. No busy city life for this guy; he's all about that serene Arctic lifestyle.

In Austria and Bavaria, "Krampusnacht" is celebrated on December 5, when the Krampus beast roams the streets. Think of it as Halloween, but with more yuletide and less candy.

🎄🎄🎄

The Philippine city of San Fernando holds the "Ligligan Parul" or Giant Lantern Festival each year, showcasing dazzling lanterns that can reach up to 20 feet in diameter. That's a lot of Christmas bulbs!

🎄🎄🎄

Armenian Orthodox Christians celebrate Christmas on January 6th, which also commemorates Jesus's baptism. Two birds, one stone.

In Japan, it's popular to eat strawberry shortcake during Christmas. No complaints here; who needs figgy pudding anyway?

🎄🎄🎄

Iceland's Yule Cat myth says that those who don't receive new clothes before Christmas would be devoured by this monstrous cat. Talk about a fashion emergency.

🎄🎄🎄

In Guatemala, on December 7th, locals sweep their houses and burn the collected dust along with effigies of the devil in a tradition called "La Quema del Diablo." Talk about a fiery spring cleaning!

Spain's "El Gordo" or "The Fat One" is a national lottery draw on December 22. It boasts the world's largest prize pool, making Christmas a little merrier for some.

🎄🎄🎄

Poland's Christmas Eve dinner, "Wigilia," serves up 12 dishes. Some say it's for the Apostles, others think it's just a year's worth of meals at once!

🎄🎄🎄

In the Caribbean, a traditional Christmas drink is sorrel punch, made from sorrel petals, ginger, and rum. Forget milk and cookies; this is what adults are leaving out for Santa.

🎄🎄🎄

The Dutch Sinterklaas sails in from Spain rather than the North Pole. Maybe he's taking a Mediterranean vacation beforehand?

In Bulgaria, Christmas Eve involves a vegetarian feast. Because even at Christmas, meatless Mondays (or in this case, possibly a meatless Friday) are a thing.

🎄🎄🎄

Mexico's "Las Posadas" is a nine-day celebration where participants re-enact Mary and Joseph's search for shelter. Spoiler alert: They eventually find a manger.

🎄🎄🎄

In South Africa it's a Christmas tradition to eat deep-fried caterpillars of the Emperor Moth. Consider it the Southern Hemisphere's answer to the Christmas pudding.

In Greece, Christmas boats are often decorated instead of trees. And yes, you're encouraged to go overboard with the decorations!

🎄🎄🎄

In Norway, there's a tradition to hide all the brooms in the house on Christmas Eve. Why? To stop the witches and mischievous spirits who come out that night from playing tricks and stealing them for a joyride!

🎄🎄🎄

In Catalonia, the "Caganer" is a popular nativity figure who is... well, let's just say he's caught mid-poo. It's a symbol of fertility and luck. Yes, you read that right.

In Malta, a Christmas Day swim is often organized to raise money for charity. The colder the swim, the warmer the heart.

🌲🌲🌲

Russian families celebrate Christmas with a 12-course dinner. Because when it comes to feasting, go big or go home.

🌲🌲🌲

In Lebanon, many people plant seeds like chickpeas, lentils, and wheat grains in cotton wool to grow by Christmas. Green thumbs have never been so festive.

🌲🌲🌲

The Colombian tradition of "La Novena" involves singing carols and prayers from December 16 to 24. It's nine nights of voice-cracking fun!

In Newfoundland, Canada, people called "Mummers" dress up in crude disguises and go from house to house dancing and playing music. It's trick-or-treating, but with less candy and more accordions.

☃ ☃ ☃

In Denmark, people traditionally jump off chairs at midnight on New Years Eve to "leap" into the New Year. It's fun until someone sprains an ankle.

☃ ☃ ☃

Estonia's Christmas sauna is a family event. Think of it as a steamy spa day, but Aunt Olga's there too!

☃ ☃ ☃

In South Korea, Christmas is often celebrated as a romantic holiday similar to Valentine's Day. Mistletoe definitely serves double duty there.

Irish families often leave mince pies and a bottle of Guinness as a treat for Santa. Maybe that's why Santa loves stopping in Ircland!

🎄🎄🎄

A Venezuelan Christmas dish, "hallaca," involves a corn dough filled with a stew of beef, pork, and chicken and wrapped in a plantain leaf. It's the turducken of tamales, swaddled in a plantain leaf!

🎄🎄🎄

Zimbabwean families celebrate Christmas with a dish called "sadza," a type of cornmeal porridge. It's the ultimate comfort food, Christmas edition.

🎄🎄🎄

In New Zealand and Australia, a summer Christmas often involves a beach barbecue. Forget roasting chestnuts; it's all about a roasting hot BBQ!

In Slovakia, the head of the household flings a piece of "lokše" potato flatbread at the ceiling on Christmas Eve. The more that sticks, the richer the crops next year. And, of course, the bigger the cleaning task afterward!

🌲🌲🌲

In France, kids leave their shoes by the fireplace, and Père Noël fills them with gifts. But beware of his sidekick, Le Père Fouettard, who brings coal.

🌲🌲🌲

In Montenegro, it's a tradition to shoot handguns into the air on Christmas Eve. Just your usual bells and, uh, bullets?

North Korean citizens could face severe punishment for celebrating Christmas, as the holiday is banned in the country. Imagine the Grinch, but way worse.

🎄🎄🎄

Greece's "Kallikantzaroi" are Christmas goblins that come out during the 12 days of Christmas. Their activities range from causing mischief to just annoying people. Sounds like some relatives we know, right?

🎄🎄🎄

Costa Ricans often decorate their homes with tropical flowers and colorful fruits during Christmas. Who needs a white Christmas when you can have a rainbow one?

In India, where only about 2.3% of the population is Christian, people often decorate mango and banana trees instead of traditional Christmas trees. It's fruity fun!

🎄🎄🎄

In Ethiopia, Christmas (or Ganna) is often celebrated with a special bread known as "Difo Dabo."

🎄🎄🎄

In Romania, Christmas is preceded by a period of fasting that lasts for 40 days, starting on November 15. So when the feast comes, it's really a feast!

🎄🎄🎄

Belgian children have not one, but two Santa figures: St. Nicholas for the French speakers and Sinterklaas for the Dutch speakers. Twice the fun or twice the confusion?

Lithuania's Christmas Eve meal, Kūčios, includes 12 dishes but no meat, dairy, or alcohol. It's like a pre-game for the indulgence that Christmas itself will bring.

🎄🎄🎄

On Christmas Day in Liberia, an offering of oil and white rice is made at church. It's both a celebration and a way to give thanks.

🎄🎄🎄

In Portugal, the Christmas meal is often enjoyed with "Bacalhau da Consoada," a traditional dish of codfish. Forget turkey or ham; fish is the star here.

In Hungary, children often receive their gifts from Baby Jesus rather than Santa Claus. Seems like the big guy outsourced some of his work.

🎄🎄🎄

Hong Kong's "WinterFest" is a fusion of East and West traditions, featuring Christmas markets, giant ornaments, and a light show across its skyscrapers. It's the city that really lights up!

🎄🎄🎄

In Serbia, for the festive season, children playfully "tie up" their parents, who then "ransom" themselves with gifts. Parent-trap, holiday edition!

🎄🎄🎄

In Armenia, children receive gifts on New Year's Day instead of Christmas. Double the holidays, double the fun!

In Egypt, Coptic Christians celebrate Christmas on January 7th. The festivities are kicked off with a special service that starts at 10 pm and ends at 4 am. Night owls rejoice!

🎄🎄🎄

In Iran, where Christians are a minority, Christmas is often celebrated quietly at home or in churches. It's a subdued, but meaningful affair.

🎄🎄🎄

In Kenya, Christmas is marked with song, dance, and nyama choma—which is similar to a BBQ. Swapping snow for sizzle, it's not your typical white Christmas!

In Scotland, Christmas was barely celebrated for about 400 years due to Protestant reforms. It only became a public holiday in 1958.

🎄🎄🎄

In Malawi, groups of children go door-to-door to perform dances and Christmas songs. They're often rewarded with little gifts, snacks, or money.

🎄🎄🎄

In Finland, some people visit cemeteries to light candles for departed loved ones, turning graveyards into peaceful seas of flickering lights.

🎄🎄🎄

Greenland celebrates Christmas with a community-wide game of soccer. It's like the World Cup, but with Santa hats.

The Bahamas has Junkanoo parades on Boxing Day and New Year's Day, where people don colorful, elaborate costumes and dance in the streets.

🎄🎄🎄

In Panama, one of the most awaited events during the Christmas season is "El Desfile de Navidad" (The Christmas Parade). This event, held in Panama City, is a nocturnal parade that features illuminated floats, marching bands, dancers, and performers, filling the streets with festive cheer and vibrant colors.

🎄🎄🎄

In Wales, "Mari Lwyd" is a horse skull mounted on a pole, carried by someone hidden under a sackcloth. It goes from house to house, engaging in a battle of rhyming insults with the occupants. That's one way to spread holiday cheer.

In Fiji, a traditional Christmas dish is "lovo," a mix of meat, fish, and vegetables cooked in a pit in the ground.

🎄🎄🎄

In Slovakia, a traditional Christmas dish is "Kapustnica," a sauerkraut soup. Who knew the holidays could be so souper?

🎄🎄🎄

In Croatia, straw is often placed under the tablecloth during the Christmas Eve feast as a reminder of the manger in Bethlehem.

🎄🎄🎄

In Slovenia, people traditionally erect nativity scenes made of moss, evergreen, and paper. It's a do-it-yourself Bethlehem.

In Ghana, a Christmas dish called "fufu" is a staple, made from root vegetables and often served with a spicy tomato soup.

🎄🎄🎄

In the Netherlands, Christmas Day is followed by a second holiday, "Tweede Kerstdag," which translates to "Second Christmas Day," and is celebrated in a similar way to Boxing Day. Because why have one when you can have two?

🎄🎄🎄

Spain's gift-giving is done primarily on January 6, Epiphany, when the Three Wise Men show up. Because the more the merrier, right?

🎄🎄🎄

Some Orthodox Churches celebrate Christmas on January 7th. They're just fashionably late to the festive fiesta.

Sources

Deutsche Welle. 2021. "Why St. Nicholas Puts Candy in Boots – DW – 12/06/2021." Dw.Com. Deutsche Welle. December 6. https://www.dw.com/en/why-st-nicholas-puts-candy-in-boots/a-18889948.

Co, Rich. 2020. "It's Christmas in the Czech Republic So Let the Shoes Fly." C&C Travel Hub. December 23. https://candctravelhub.wordpress.com/2020/12/23/christmas-in-the-czech-republic-shoes/.

"The Ukrainian Tradition of Spider Webs and Christmas." 2018. Ukraine. Com. September 21. https://www.ukraine.com/blog/spiders-and-their-webs-are-not-showed-the-door-on-ukrainian-christmas/.

"Christmas in Ethiopia." 2023. Brilliant Ethiopia. Accessed September 27. https://www.brilliant-ethiopia.com/christmas-in-ethiopia.

"Kiviak." 2023. Wikipedia. Wikimedia Foundation. June 17. https://en.wikipedia.org/wiki/Kiviak.

"Christmas In Portugal." 2023. World Of Christmas. Accessed September 27. http://www.worldofchristmas.net/christmas-world/portugal.html.

"About the Gävle Goat." 2023. Visit Gävle. Accessed September 27. https://www.visitgavle.se/en/about-gavle-goat.

20/12/2019, Debra Thimmesch |, Debra Thimmesch, and Author name Debra Thimmesch. 2023. "The Legend of La Befana." ItaliaRail. Accessed September 27. https://www.italiarail.com/culture/legend-la-befana.

"Joulupukki." 2023. Wikipedia. Wikimedia Foundation. September 9. https://en.wikipedia.org/wiki/Joulupukki.

"Krampus." 2023. Wikipedia. Wikimedia Foundation. September 19. https://en.wikipedia.org/wiki/Krampus.

"Who We Are?" 2023. Giant Lantern. Accessed September 27. https://giant-lanterns.com/about/.

"Why Do Armenians Celebrate Christmas on January 6th?" 2023. Diocese of The Armenian Church. Accessed September 27. https://armenianchurch.org.uk/why-do-armenians-celebrate-christmas-on-january-6th/.

Bruzek, Alison. 2014. "Japan's Beloved Christmas Cake Isn't About Christmas At All." NPR. NPR. December 16. https://www.npr.org/sections/thesalt/2014/12/16/369830094/a-christmas-cake-that-isn-t-about-christmas-at-all.

"Icelandic Christmas Folklore." 2023. Wikipedia. Wikimedia Foundation. September 27. https://en.wikipedia.org/wiki/Icelandic_Christmas_folklore.

Aroche, Karin. 2021. "Hoy Se Celebra La Tradición de La Quema Del Diablo En Guatemala." Aprende Guatemala.Com. December 1. https://aprende.guatemala.com/cultura-guatemalteca/tradiciones/quema-del-diablo-en-guatemala/.

Deutsche Welle. 2021. "Spain Holds Draw for World's Richest Lottery – DW – 12/22/2021." Dw.Com. Deutsche Welle. December 22. https://www.dw.com/en/el-gordo-spain-holds-draw-for-worlds-richest-lottery/a-60221600.

"Wigilia." 2023. Wikipedia. Wikimedia Foundation. April 29. https://en.wikipedia.org/wiki/Wigilia.

Atkinson, Jillian. 2023. "In Jamaica, Christmas Isn't Complete Without Tart, Gingery Sorrel." Serious Eats. Serious Eats. August 24. https://www.seriouseats.com/jamaican-sorrel-hibiscus-drink.

O'Connor, Coilin, and Teodora Barzakova. 2020. "Christmas In Bulgaria: 'You Basically Become Vegan For 40 Days.'" RadioFreeEurope/RadioLiberty. Radio Free Europe / Radio Liberty. December 24. https://www.rferl.org/a/bulgaria-christmas-vegan-food-traditions-pitka-koledari-kapama/31010447.html.

2023. Twinkl.Es. Accessed September 27. https://www.twinkl.es/teaching-wiki/las-posadas-for-kids.

Holidays, Author Avatar Post written by:Newmarket, Author Avatar, and Post written by:Newmarket Holidays. 2022. "Cultural Christmas Traditions Worldwide: Newmarket Holidays." Newmarket Holidays. https://www.newmarketholidays.co.uk/blog/cultural-christmas-traditions

Atlanticyachtandship. 2017. "The Christmas Boat, an Old Greek Tradition Still Thriving Today." Atlantic Yacht And Ship. December 14. https://atlanticyachtandship.com/christmas-boat-greek-tradition.

Culturetrip. 2023. "What Is the Caganer the 'Defecating' Catalan..." Culture Trip. September 27. https://theculturetrip.com/europe/spain/articles/everything-you-need-to-know-about-the-catalan-caganer.

Meridith. 2018. "Leave Swimsuits Within Easy Reach - The Thomas Smith Charity Swim Is Back." Thomas Smith Insurance Agency. November 14. https://www.tcsmithinsurance.com/blog/thomas-smith-charity-swim-back-2018.

"Christmas Eve." 2023. Advantour. Accessed September 27. https://www.advantour.com/russia/traditions/christmas-eve.htm.

Kehdy, Bethany. 2019. "How We Celebrate Christmas in Lebanon." Kitchn. Apartment Therapy, LLC. May 2. https://www.thekitchn.com/how-we-celebrate-christmas-in-lebanon-christmas-around-the-world-198480.

Sánchez, Karen. 2022. "¿Cómo y Por Qué Se Celebra La Novena de Aguinaldos En Colombia?" Voz de América. Voz de América. December 20. https://www.vozdeamerica.com/a/como-celebra-novena-aguinaldos-colombia-/6883132.html.

Laskow, Sarah. 2022. "Newfoundland's Mummering Tradition Is the Oldest and Creepiest in North America." Atlas Obscura. Atlas Obscura. December 6. https://www.atlasobscura.com/articles/the-longbanned-tradition-of-mummering-in-newfoundland-is-making-a-comeback.

"11 Weird Traditions That Only Make Sense to Danes." 2023. VisitDenmark. Accessed September 27. https://www.visitdenmark.com/denmark/things-do/danish-culture/danish-traditions.

Estonian World. 2022. "Christmas Traditions in Estonia." Estonian World. December 23. https://estonianworld.com/life/christmas-customs-estonia/.
"A Couple's Paradise: Christmas in South Korea." 2020. KoreanClass101.Com Blog. December 10. https://www.koreanclass101.com/blog/2020/12/10/christmas-in-south-korea/.

"Irish Traditions." 2023. Byers Choice. Accessed September 27. https://www.byerschoice.com/christmas-traditions/ireland.

Knelly, Clarice. 2022. "Why Venezuela's Hallaca Is Pretty Much Only Made During The Holidays." Tasting Table. Tasting Table. November 27. https://www.tastingtable.com/1115107/why-venezuelas-hallaca-is-pretty-much-only-made-during-the-holidays.

"Christmas in Zimbabwe." 2023. WorldRemit. Accessed September 27. https://www.worldremit.com/en/blog/community/christmas-in-zimbabwe. Co, Rich. 2020. "Christmas in Slovakia Means Loksa on the Ceiling." C&C Travel Hub. December 16. https://candctravelhub.wordpress.com/2020/12/16/christmas-slovakia-loksa-ceiling/.

Alpine French School. 2022. "French Christmas Traditions." Alpine French School. December 20. https://alpinefrenchschool.com/blog/some-french-christmas-traditions.

Culturetrip. 2023. "How to Celebrate Christmas in Montenegro." Culture Trip. September 27. https://theculturetrip.com/europe/montenegro/articles/how-to-celebrate-christmas-in-montenegro.

Tambini, Joe. 2017. "Kim Jong-Un BANS Christmas: Why Doesn't North Korea Have Christmas?" Express.Co.Uk. Express.co.uk. December 23. https://www.express.co.uk/news/world/896055/North-Korea-news-Christmas-celebrate-Kim-Jong-un-ban.

"Kallikantzaros." 2023. Wikipedia. Wikimedia Foundation. September 21. https://en.wikipedia.org/wiki/Kallikantzaros.

Olenakagui. 2020. "Christmas in India: Decorated Mango Trees & 'Christmas Baba.'" The Travel Bug Bite. March 28. https://thetravelbugbite.com/2019/12/18/christmas-in-india/.

Andreitzale, Published. 2022. "If You Love Tradition, You Need To Spend Christmas In Romania." Beyond Dracula. December 30. https://www.beyond-dracula.com/christmas-in-romania/.

"Kūčios (Christmas Eve)." 2023. Lithuania Travel. Accessed September 27. https://www.lithuania.travel/en/news/kucios-christmas-eve.

Leite, David. 2023. "Christmas Eve Cod ~ Bacalhau Da Consoada." Leite's Culinaria. June 12. https://leitesculinaria.com/7651/recipes-portuguese-christmas-eve-cod.html.

JPC-DESIGN, whychristmas?com /. 2023. "Christmas in Hungary on Whychristmas?Com." Why Christmas. Accessed September 27. https://www.whychristmas.com/cultures/hungary.

"Hong Kong WinterFest: Hong Kong Tourism Board." 2023. Discover Hong Kong. Accessed September 27. https://www.discoverhongkong.com/eng/what-s-new/events/dhk-highlighted-events/hong-kong-winterfest.html.

"Christmas in Serbia." 2023. Wikipedia. Wikimedia Foundation. September 24. https://en.wikipedia.org/wiki/Christmas_in_Serbia.

Christin. 2018. "Armenian New Year Ancient Traditions - Levon Travel." Levon-travel.Am. November 22. https://www.levontravel.am/armenian-new-year-traditions/.

Birtles, Katie. 2023. "Christmas in Egypt, Where Everyone's Favourite Holiday Is Celebrated Twice." Real Word. July 24. https://www.trafalgar.com/real-word/christmas-egypt-celebrated-twice/.

Zeinali, Frida. 2020. "Christmas, Quietly Observed, In Iran." Youth Journalism International. December 4. https://youthjournalism.org/christmas-quietly-observed-in-iran/.

Birtles, Katie. 2020. "Heri Ya Krismasi - How Christmas Is Celebrated in Kenya." Real Word. December 1. https://www.trafalgar.com/real-word/how-christmas-kenya-celebrated/.

"Scottish Christmas Traditions." 1970. The University of Edinburgh. May 9. https://www.ed.ac.uk/medicine-vet-medicine/postgraduate/postgraduate-blog/scottish-christmas-traditions

Roberts, Maddy Shaw, and Rosie Pentreath. 2021. "Which Countries Have Christmas Carols as a Tradition – and What Are the Best Carols from around the World?" Classic FM. Classic FM. December 17. https://www.classicfm.com/discover-music/occasions/christmas/world-best-international-carols/.

Aucor. 2020. "Christmas Eve in a Candlelit Finnish Cemetery." thisisFINLAND. December 10. https://finland.fi/christmas/christmas-eve-in-a-candlelit-cemetery/.

"Junkanoo - Annual Events in The Bahamas." 2023. The Islands of The Bahamas. Accessed September 27. https://www.bahamas.com/events/junkanoo.

"The Mari Lwyd." 2023. Wales. Accessed September 27. https://www.wales. com/about/culture/mari-lwyd.

2023. Curiosidades Del Desfile de Navidad |. Accessed September 27. https:// mupa.gob.pa/curiosidades-del-desfile-de-navidad/.

Arylic, and Instructables. 2017. "Do a 'Lovo' for Christmas : Fijian Style." Instructables. Instructables. November 9. https://www.instructables.com/Do-a-quotLovoquot-For-christmas-Fijian-Style/.

Rhianon, and Name. 2016. "Slovak Recipes Worth Taking Home: Kapustnica (Sauerkraut Soup)." Bratislava Food Tours. August 4. https://bratislavafood-tours.com/slovak-recipes-worth-taking-home-kapustnica-sauerkraut-soup/

Kubilius, Kerry. 2019. "These Traditions Will Help You Celebrate a Croatian-Style Christmas." TripSavvy. TripSavvy. February 12. https://www.tripsavvy.com/croatia-christmas-traditions-1501178

Ceferin, Aleksandra. 2017. "Jaslice – The Manger in Slovenian Christmas Tradition." Thezaurus.Com - Generation Next. December 2. https://thezaurus. com/jaslice-the-manger-in-slovenian-christmas-tradition/.

"Tweede Kerstdag." 2022. Wikipedia. Wikimedia Foundation. December 26. https://nl.wikipedia.org/wiki/Tweede_kerstdag.

The Science of Christmas

Lights, chemistry, and holiday spirit—oh my! When tinsel meets test tubes, you get the fascinating Science of Christmas. Ever wondered why snowflakes are unique? Or what triggers that warm, fuzzy "holiday spirit" in our brains? Behind the mistletoe kisses and the shimmering lights, there's a world of scientific wonders waiting to be explored. In this chapter, we'll delve deep into the wintry phenomena, explore the psychology behind our festive feelings, and unravel the tech that lights up our trees.

So, strap on your lab goggles, and prepare to see the holiday season in a whole new (LED) light!

Feeling generous during Christmas? Blame it on oxytocin, the "love hormone," which is released when we hug or give gifts. Science just explained your urge to buy that extra gift!

🎁 🎁 🎁

Studies show that Christmas music can genuinely make some people happier due to the release of dopamine. So go ahead, blast "All I Want for Christmas is You" guilt-free.

🎁 🎁 🎁

Snowflakes are hexagonal due to the molecular structure of water. Six sides, infinite coolness!

🎁 🎁 🎁

LED Christmas lights use up to 75% less energy than their incandescent counterparts. It's like giving Mother Earth a present.

The record for the most lights on a Christmas tree stands at 612,000, achieved in Japan in 2022. That's brighter than my future.

🎁 🎁 🎁

Reindeer have specialized noses that warm the cold air before it gets to their lungs. So, under a thermal camera, Rudolph's nose really is red!

🎁 🎁 🎁

Ever wonder why Christmas colors are red and green? Color psychologists think it's because red arouses and excites, while green is calming. Emotional rollercoaster, anyone?

🎁 🎁 🎁

A study found that people who put up Christmas decorations earlier, were happier. Now you have a scientific excuse for decking the halls in September!

You know how snow crunches underfoot? That's because you're compressing the air between snowflakes, making a mini snow symphony.

🎁 🎁 🎁

"Flocking" a Christmas tree means spraying it white to simulate snow. The process involves cellulose fibers. DIY winter wonderland!

🎁 🎁 🎁

Poinsettias, the Christmas flower, react to light cycles. To make them turn red, they need darkness for at least 14 hours a day for 6 weeks. They're basically the vampires of the plant world.

🎁 🎁 🎁

Real Christmas trees consume about a quart of water per day. They're like a sponge at a water fight!

Studies have shown that the smell of pine needles can actually reduce stress. So, if you're freaking out over holiday shopping, just sniff a Christmas tree.

🎁 🎁 🎁

The word "mistletoe" actually means "dung twig" in ancient languages. Let that sink in next time you're going in for a kiss.

🎁 🎁 🎁

The North Pole is warmer than the South Pole, with average winter temperatures around -34°F compared to the South's chilling -76°F. Santa chose wisely.

Older Christmas lights operated in a series circuit, so when one bulb went out, the whole string went dark. Modern designs, however, have evolved to keep the holiday cheer going even if a bulb takes a break.

🎁 🎁 🎁

The shortest day of the year, the Winter Solstice, often falls around Christmas. No wonder we need all those twinkling lights to brighten things up!

🎁 🎁 🎁

The "Christmas Star" phenomenon involves the close alignment of planets, like Jupiter and Saturn, creating a bright point in the sky. The most recent occurrence was on December 21, 2020, which was the first time in 800 years.

The reason why we put tinsel on Christmas trees comes from an old German legend about spiders whose web turned into silver when spun around a Christmas tree. The real science? The transformation of raw materials into silver tinsel through aluminum-based production!

🎁 🎁 🎁

Reindeer eyes change color in the winter to adapt to lower light levels, going from gold to blue. It's their own festive mood ring.

🎁 🎁 🎁

On the psychological front, the "Scrooge Effect" refers to the idea that thinking about death during Christmas can make people more generous. Spooky but sweet?

There's a scientific name for the fear of Christmas: "Christougenniatikophobia." Try saying that three times fast.

🎁 🎁 🎁

Research shows nearly half of all women feel stress during the holiday season. The culprits? Gift-giving, family gatherings, and financial strain. Even joy comes with fine print.

🎁 🎁 🎁

The "warm" light of incandescent bulbs is due to the color temperature being around 2,700 Kelvin. Your cozy feels are actually measurable!

🎁 🎁 🎁

"SAD" or Seasonal Affective Disorder affects many during winter. The prescription? More exposure to light, which makes Christmas lights doubly beneficial.

According to a study, people are more likely to die on Christmas Day than any other day of the year, often from natural causes. The reasons aren't entirely clear, but potential factors might include staffing changes at hospitals and the emotional stress of holidays.

🎁 🎁 🎁

Research shows that people born in December live longer and are more likely to reach 105+. Another reason to celebrate your Christmas birthday!

Snow is an insulator because it traps air in between its flakes. This is why igloos are warmer than you'd think.

🎁 🎁 🎁

When it's very cold and calm, large snowflakes can form. When it's slightly warmer and the wind is strong, snowflakes are smaller. Choose your winter wonderland!

🎁 🎁 🎁

Real Christmas trees are more environmentally friendly than artificial ones if recycled properly. Also, they don't collect dust in your attic.

While flying through the sky, Santa and his reindeer would have to deal with speeds that could cause a "sonic boom." Forget sleigh bells, imagine breaking the sound barrier!

🎁 🎁 🎁

The melting point of snow depends not just on temperature but also on the presence of impurities like dirt or other particles. Snow is a picky melter.

🎁 🎁 🎁

The Fraser fir holds onto its needles like it's clinging to the holiday spirit, while the Eastern Red Cedar drops them faster than hot cocoa on a snowy day. Choose wisely for a less prickly January!

Real Christmas trees produce oxygen. An acre of Christmas trees can produce enough O^2 for 18 people per day. Take that, artificial trees!

🎁 🎁 🎁

There's a phenomenon called "Thundersnow," which is a snowstorm with thunder and lightning. It's like a heavy metal version of Christmas.

🎁 🎁 🎁

When snow falls, it actually absorbs sound, making everything seem quieter. It's nature's mute button.

🎁 🎁 🎁

Eggnog was originally believed to be a health tonic. Given its combination of eggs, milk, and alcohol, it was like the protein shake of the 1700s.

According to physics, thanks to time zones and Earth's rotation, Santa has a whopping 31 hours to work his Christmas magic. Traveling east to west, he'd have to visit 822.6 homes every second, giving him a mere 1/1000th of a second for each stop! Crunching the numbers, this means his sleigh speeds around at a blistering 650 miles per second. That's 3,000 times faster than sound and vastly outpaces the Ulysses space probe, our fastest man-made vehicle. Talk about turbocharged reindeer!

🎁 🎁 🎁

The red and green shades of Christmas lights have wavelengths of approximately 700 and 530 nanometers, respectively. Finally, a legitimate reason to discuss wavelengths at Christmas dinner!

The Christingle combines spiritual symbolism with our brain's natural inclination to recognize patterns and find meaning. An orange represents the world, a candle illustrates Jesus's light, and fruits and nuts signify God's creations. It's not just a spiritual ritual; it's a nod to how our brains are wired for symbolism!

🎁 🎁 🎁

Because of the Coriolis Effect, snowstorms spin counterclockwise in the Northern Hemisphere and clockwise in the Southern Hemisphere. It's like nature's dreidel!

🎁 🎁 🎁

Research has shown that peppermint can actually improve cognitive functions. Eating candy canes is basically brain training.

Want to calculate the height of your Christmas tree? Use the "Mirror Method," a simple trigonometric approach. All you need is a mirror, a ruler, and a dash of holiday spirit.

🎁 🎁 🎁

The Leidenfrost effect explains why you can wet your fingers and briefly touch hot Christmas pudding without getting burned. The Leidenfrost effect occurs when a liquid comes into contact with a surface significantly hotter than the liquid's boiling point. The immediate vaporization creates an insulating vapor layer that prevents the liquid from boiling away quickly. It's not magic; it's thermodynamics!

🎁 🎁 🎁

The shiniest tinsel is made of Mylar, a polyester film. It's chemically stable, so you won't tarnish the holiday spirit.

Ever wonder how many calories you burn wrapping gifts? Around 120 calories per hour! No wonder it feels like a workout.

🎁 🎁 🎁

Fruitcakes can last for years thanks to their high sugar content, acting as a preservative. When the apocalypse comes, it'll be cockroaches and fruitcakes that survive.

🎁 🎁 🎁

Research from National Institutes of Health suggests that "holiday weight gain" is largely a myth. The average gain is just around 1 pound. So have that second helping!

Tinsel was originally made from shredded silver. Thanks to oxidation, it often turned black and tarnished the holiday spirit—literally!

🎁 🎁 🎁

Snow is white because it reflects all the colors in the spectrum equally. It's the Swiss army knife of weather phenomena.

🎁 🎁 🎁

People who suffer from "ornithophobia" might struggle during Christmas, thanks to the "12 Days of Christmas" song featuring so many birds. Partridges, turtle doves, French hens, calling birds...

Evergreen trees have needles containing a type of protein that works as an antifreeze. They were surviving harsh winters way before your car was!

🎁 🎁 🎁

Wreaths date back to the Roman Empire where they were a symbol of victory. Science can't explain why your neighbor's wreath is still up in July, though.

🎁 🎁 🎁

Psychologists say singing carols can reduce stress. But the jury is still out on how your off-key renditions impact others.

Research shows that a sugar high from Christmas cookies doesn't actually make kids hyperactive. Looks like you'll need another excuse for their boundless energy.

🎁 🎁 🎁

If you shake a snow globe, the snowflakes inside swirl around due to fluid dynamics and gravity, creating a mini blizzard in a bubble. It's physics, not just festive fun!

🎁 🎁 🎁

Artificial snow for movie sets can be made using a variety of substances, including cornflakes painted white. Hollywood's snow isn't just flakey in the metaphorical sense.

"First-footing" is a New Year's custom in Scotland of bringing coal, bread, and salt to a home to ensure warmth, food, and flavor for the coming year. It's an early form of wealth distribution, just more tasty.

🎁 🎁 🎁

Want to know why we toast with drinks? Well, no one really knows! There are many theories, including one about warding off evil spirits with the sound or to check for poison. Today, we toast to celebrate shared moments and camaraderie. Cheers to good vibes and science!

🎁 🎁 🎁

In Victorian times, engineers constructed "ice palaces" as a display of skill. Your snowman suddenly seems a little underwhelming, doesn't it?

Studies show that cold weather can actually sharpen your mind. So, no excuses for forgetting where you hid that last Christmas present!

🎁 🎁 🎁

Some claim it's possible to wrap a gift with just two pieces of tape. If you've ever done it with twenty, don't worry; you're not alone.

🎁 🎁 🎁

During the 1965 Gemini VI mission, astronauts Tom Stafford and Wally Schirra played a prank where they reported seeing a UFO which turned out to be Santa Claus and then played "Jingle Bells" on a harmonica accompanied by sleigh bells.

Kissing under the mistletoe could be healthy! Mistletoe berries have compounds used in cancer research. Just don't swallow them; they're toxic in large amounts.

🎁 🎁 🎁

The term Yule log could be derived from the Norse word 'jol,' which refers to a 12-day festival celebrating the winter solstice. It's not just a delicious cake; it's a history lesson.

🎁 🎁 🎁

Glögg, a traditional Scandinavian mulled wine, is often made with a combination of spices like cloves, cardamom, and cinnamon, and then fortified with either brandy or vodka. In Sweden, it's often served with raisins and almonds and is a staple at Christmas markets and gatherings.

Artificial snow in a can contains a polymer called sodium polyacrylate, which can absorb up to 300 times its mass in water. That's like a sponge on steroids.

🎁 🎁 🎁

According to a 2016 study, receiving experiential gifts, like a cooking class, generates more happiness than material ones. Science says your Christmas shopping list just got easier.

🎁 🎁 🎁

During winter, the Earth is actually closer to the Sun due to its elliptical orbit. It's not the Earth that's avoiding the Sun; it's the tilt!

Psychologists theorize that the reason we love the coziness of Christmas may be linked to the Danish concept of "hygge," which promotes comfort and contentment.

🎁 🎁 🎁

Some psychologists believe the reason we find Christmas lights so captivating is due to our primitive attraction to fire. It's like a caveman rave.

Sources

"What Happens in Your Brain When You Give a Gift?" 2023. American Psychological Association. American Psychological Association. Accessed September 27. https://www.apa.org/topics/mental-health/brain-gift-giving.

AMG, Scripps. 2023. "Holiday Music Can Make You Healthier • Scripps AMG." Scripps Affiliated Medical Groups. May 19. https://scrippsamg.com/holiday-music-can-make-you-healthier/.

"Snowflakes." 2014. Young People's Trust For the Environment. September 15. https://ypte.org.uk/factsheets/snowflakes/what-gives-snowflakes-their-shape.

"Incandescent vs. LED Christmas Lights." 2023. YEELIGHT. YEELIGHT. June 16. https://store.yeelight.com/blogs/everything-about-lights/incandescent-vs-led-christmas-lights.

"Most Lights on an Artificial Christmas Tree." 2023. Guinness World Records. Accessed September 27. https://www.guinnessworldrecords.com/world-records/97811-most-lights-on-an-artificial-christmas-tree.

Olson, Eric R. 2021. "Snowbound: Animals of Winter - Reindeer Noses Really Do Glow Red." PBS. Public Broadcasting Service. December 30. https://www.pbs.org/wnet/nature/reindeer-noses-really-glow-red/14868/.

TodayShow. 2022. "The History and Meaning behind Traditional Christmas Colors." TODAY.Com. TODAY. December 1. https://www.today.com/life/holidays/christmas-colors-rcna59377.

"People Who Put up Christmas Decorations Early Are Happier." 2017. The Independent. Independent Digital News and Media. November 21. https://www.independent.co.uk/life-style/people-put-christmas-decorations-up-early-happier-feelings-stress-anxiety-december-experts-study-a8065561.html.

"Why Is Snow So Noisy Underfoot? The Science Behind That Crunchy Sound." 2023. WTTW News. Accessed September 27. https://news.wttw.com/2021/02/16/why-snow-so-noisy-underfoot-science-behind-crunchy-sound.

VanSchmus, Emily. 2022. "How to Flock a Christmas Tree for a Festive Snow-Covered Look." Better Homes & Gardens. Better Homes & Gardens. November 15. https://www.bhg.com/christmas/trees/how-to-flock-a-tree-two-ways/.

Vanstone, Emma. 2022. "Why Are Poinsettias Red?" Science Experiments for Kids. December 30. https://www.science-sparks.com/why-are-poinsettias-red/#:~:text=Poinsettias%20are%20photoperiodic.,them%20their%20bright%20red%20colour.

Bill Lindberg, Michigan State University Extension. 2022. "Making Your Real Christmas Tree Last through the Holidays." Christmas Trees. November 16. https://www.canr.msu.edu/news/water_is_the_essential_ingredient_in_keeping_your_farm_grown_christmas_tree.

Sonyadibbin. 2022. "Benefits of Pine: 5 Reasons to Love Our Precious Pines." Adore Your Outdoors. November 2. https://adoreyouroutdoors.co.uk/pine-tree-benefits/.

Hiskey, Daven. 2014. "Why We Kiss Under the Mistletoe." Today I Found Out. December 5. http://www.todayifoundout.com/index.php/2010/12/the-word-mistletoe-literally-means-dung-twig/.

Choi, Charles Q. 2022. "Which Is Colder: The North or South Pole?" LiveScience. Purch. June 5. https://www.livescience.com/is-north-pole-or-south-pole-colder#:~:text=The%20annual%20average%20temperature%20at,minus%2028.2%20C)%20in%20summer.

"Winter Solstice." 2023. Wikipedia. Wikimedia Foundation. July 13. https://en.wikipedia.org/wiki/Winter_solstice.

Carter, Jamie. 2021. "A Spectacularly Rare 'Christmas Star' Is Coming In December As Two Worlds Align After Sunset." Forbes. Forbes Magazine. December 10. https://www.forbes.com/sites/jamiecartereurope/2020/11/20/a-spectacularly-rare-christmas-star-is-coming-in-december-as-two-worlds-align-after-sunset/.

Borunda, Alejandra. 2022. "What Color Are Reindeer Eyes? Depends on the Season." Animals. National Geographic. December 20. https://www.nationalgeographic.com/animals/article/reindeer-eyes-color-change-season-uv.

"APA PsycNet." 2023. American Psychological Association. American Psychological Association. Accessed September 27. https://psycnet.apa.org/record/2002-18574-004.

Bababam. 2023. "Do You Really Know?: What Is Christougenniatikopho-bia? En Apple Podcasts." Apple Podcasts. Accessed September 27. https://podcasts.apple.com/ni/podcast/what-is-christougenniatikophobia/id1490875304?i=1000546636414.

"APA Survey Shows Holiday Stress Putting Women's Health at Risk." 2023. American Psychological Association. American Psychological Association. Accessed September 27. https://www.apa.org/news/press/releases/2006/12/women-stress.

Staff, Waveform. 2019. "Choosing Between 2700K and 3000K." Waveform Lighting. Waveform Lighting. March 21. https://www.waveformlighting.com/home-residential/choosing-between-2700k-and-3000k.

professional, Cleveland Clinic medical. 2023. "Seasonal Depression (Seasonal Affective Disorder)." Cleveland Clinic. Accessed September 27. https://my.clevelandclinic.org/health/diseases/9293-seasonal-depression.

Ucl. 2022. "Reindeer Use UV Light to Survive in the Wild." UCL News. May 6. https://www.ucl.ac.uk/news/2011/may/reindeer-use-uv-light-survive-wild.

"Shelter and Insulation." 2023. Our Winter World. Accessed September 27. http://ourwinterworld.org/snow-and-living-things/animals/shelter-and-insulation.

"People Born in December Are Smarter and Tend to Live Longer, a Study Suggests." 2019. Bright Side - Inspiration. Creativity. Wonder. Bright Side. December 12. https://brightside.me/articles/people-born-in-december-are-smarter-and-tend-to-live-longer-study-suggests-795070/.

"Here's Why Snowflakes Can Be Large or Small." 2023. Weather Underground. Accessed September 27. https://www.wunderground.com/article/safety/winter/news/2020-02-10-snowflake-size-difference-large-wet-small-dry.

"Real vs. Fake-Which Christmas Tree Is Better for the Environment?" 2019. The Nature Conservancy. December 2. https://www.nature.org/en-us/what-we-do/our-priorities/protect-water-and-land/land-and-water-stories/real-vs-fake-christmas-tree

Leonid A. Dombrovsky. "The Influence of Pollution on Solar Heating and Melting of a Snowpack." Journal of Quantitative Spectroscopy and Radiative Transfer. Pergamon. May 14. https://www.sciencedirect.com/science/article/abs/pii/S0022407319302390.

"10 Surprising Facts About Christmas Trees." 2023. Heritage Radio Network. Accessed September 27. https://heritageradionetwork.org/10-surprising-facts-about-christmas-trees.

Hollister, Debbie, Stephanie Rose, and Sheila. 2023. "How to Pick the Best Type of Christmas Tree for Your Family." Garden Therapy. March 22. https://gardentherapy.ca/pick-the-best-christmas-tree.

"Thundersnow." 2023. Wikipedia. Wikimedia Foundation. September 10. https://en.wikipedia.org/wiki/Thundersnow.

Cleveland, Claire, and Andrea Dukakis. 2023. "Yes, It Really Is Quieter When It Snows. Here's The Science Behind The Calm After The Storm." Colorado Public Radio. Colorado Public Radio. https://www.cpr.org/2020/02/04/yes-it-really-is-quieter-when-it-snows-heres-the-science-behind-the-calm-after-the-storm/.

"EggNog in History, Health, and Hospitality – Circulating Now from the NLM Historical Collections." 2023. U.S. National Library of Medicine. National Institutes of Health. Accessed September 27. https://circulatingnow.nlm.nih.gov/2022/12/22/eggnog-in-history-health-and-hospitality/.

2023. Santa. Accessed September 27. https://www.mit.edu/people/dmredish/wwwMLRF/links/Humor/Existance_of_Santa.html.

"The Visible Spectrum." 2023. Encyclopædia Britannica. Encyclopædia Britannica, inc. Accessed September 27. https://www.britannica.com/science/color/The-visible-spectrum.

"The History Of The Christingle." 2023. The History Of The Christingle | Out of the Ark Blog | Out of the Ark Music. Accessed September 27. https://www.outoftheark.co.uk/blog/the-history-of-the-christingle/.

"The Coriolis Effect: Earth's Rotation and Its Effect on Weather." 2023. Education. Accessed September 27. https://education.nationalgeographic.org/resource/coriolis-effect/.

K;, Moss M;Hewitt S;Moss L;Wesnes. 2023. "Modulation of Cognitive Performance and Mood by Aromas of Peppermint and Ylang-Ylang." The International Journal of Neuroscience. U.S. National Library of Medicine. Accessed September 27. https://pubmed.ncbi.nlm.nih.gov/18041606.

"Exploring the Leidenfrost Effect." 2023. COMSOL. Accessed September 27. https://www.comsol.com/blogs/leidenfrost-effect.

"Tinsel." 2023. Wikipedia. Wikimedia Foundation. August 14. https://en.wikipedia.org/wiki/Tinsel.

"10 Unusual Ways to Burn Christmas Calories." Real Buzz. https://www.realbuzz.com/articles-interests/festive-health-fitness/article/10-unusual-ways-to-burn-calories/

"Holiday Weight Gain a Big Fat Lie." 2023. WebMD. WebMD. Accessed September 27. https://www.webmd.com/diet/features/holiday-weight-gain-big-fat-lie.

Oblack, Rachelle. 2019. "What Makes Snow White?" ThoughtCo. ThoughtCo. December 1. https://www.thoughtco.com/why-is-snow-white-3444537.

"Why Pines Are Evergreen." 2023. EarthDate. Accessed September 27. https://www.earthdate.org/episodes/why-pines-are-evergreen.

Tejada, Chloe. 2019. "Singing Carols Can Boost More Than Just Your Holiday Cheer." HuffPost. HuffPost. December 23. https://www.huffpost.com/archive/ca/entry/singing-christmas-music_ca_5defbd5fe4b00563b858662b.

Carruthers, Tom. 2017. "Does Sugar Really Make Kids Hyper?" Curious. October 23. https://www.science.org.au/curious/people-medicine/does-sugar-really-make-kids-hyper.

"Snow Globe Dynamics." 2014. Cavmaths. July 4. https://cavmaths.wordpress.com/2014/05/29/snow-globe-dynamics/.

Author Maureen Lee Lenker   By Maureen Lee Lenker November 17, 2021 at 10:30 AM EST. 2023. "How 'It's a Wonderful Life' Devised a New Form of Fake Snow That Revolutionized the Medium." EW.Com. Accessed September 27. https://ew.com/movies/its-a-wonderful-life-fake-snow.

"First Footing." 2022. Revels. https://revels.org/cultural_traditions/first-footing.

Hauntedmontreal. 2021. "Hauntedmontreal." Haunted Montreal. February 13. https://hauntedmontreal.com/haunted-montreal-blog-66-montreals-haunted-victorian-era-ice-castles.html.

Jarrett, Christian. 2016. "Your Brain Performs Better When It's Cold Outside." CNN. Cable News Network. February 19. https://edition.cnn.com/2016/02/19/health/your-brain-on-winter/index.html.

Space Coast Daily. 2017. "THIS DAY IN HISTORY: Gemini VI Crew Pull Christmas Prank, First Song Performed In Space." Space Coast Daily. December 16. https://spacecoastdaily.com/2017/12/this-day-in-history-gemini-vi-crew-pull-christmas-prank-first-song-performed-in-space/.

Patel, Seema, and Suryakanta Panda. 2014. "Emerging Roles of Mistletoes in Malignancy Management." 3 Biotech. U.S. National Library of Medicine. February 1. https://www.ncbi.nlm.nih.gov/pmc/articles/PMC3909578.

Brady, M. Michael. 2021. "Yule - Jul ." The Norwegian American. December 21. https://www.norwegianamerican.com/yule-jul/.

"'Artificial Snow' Experiment." 2023. MEL Science. Accessed September 27. https://melscience.com/ES-en/articles/artificial-snow-experiment.

"Why Experiences Are Better Gifts than Things." 2022. Follow Alice. July 13. https://followalice.com/knowledge/why-experiences-are-better-gifts-than-things.

"Danish Hygge." 2023. Denmark.Dk. Accessed September 27. https://denmark.dk/people-and-culture/hygge.

Christmas Classics

Lights, camera, festive action! There's nothing quite like snuggling up with a heartwarming Christmas classic, be it a timeless film, a soul-stirring carol, or a literary masterpiece. But what's the story behind these iconic holiday treasures? How did they come to define the very essence of the Christmas season for so many of us?

In this chapter, we'll journey through snowy film sets, crooning recording studios, and ink-stained pages to uncover the magic behind the classics.

While George Bailey's story in "It's a Wonderful Life" is heartwarming, the movie was initially a box-office flop. It didn't become popular until it entered the public domain and was played repeatedly on TV.

"A Christmas Carol" by Charles Dickens was published on December 19, 1843, and sold out within five days. If Dickens were alive today, he'd probably have a killer Instagram account.

"Jingle Bells" was originally penned by James Lord Pierpont in 1857 for Thanksgiving. The song switched teams and now we can't think of it as anything but a Christmas jam.

Believe it or not, "White Christmas" by Irving Berlin is the best-selling single of all time, moving over 50 million copies since 1942. Bing Crosby sure knows how to belt out a holiday hit!

"Rudolph the Red-Nosed Reindeer" was created as a promotional figure for Montgomery Ward department stores. So yes, Rudolph was born from capitalism, not a reindeer mom.

Dr. Seuss wrote "How the Grinch Stole Christmas!" in just a few weeks. It's taken me longer to assemble some IKEA furniture.

"A Charlie Brown Christmas" was considered a project doomed to fail by its own creators. Imagine their surprise when half the TVs in the U.S. tuned in to watch it on December 9, 1965!

In "Home Alone," the photo of Buzz's girlfriend is actually a picture of a boy made to look like a girl. The filmmakers thought making fun of a girl would be too cruel. Kudos for sensitivity?

"The Polar Express" was the first movie to be entirely shot using motion capture technology. Tom Hanks plays six roles in it. Six!

"Frosty the Snowman" debuted as a song before it became an animated TV special in 1969.

Frank Capra, the director of "It's a Wonderful Life," didn't see the film as a Christmas movie. It was initially a response to the cynicism he saw post-World War II.

The poem "The Night Before Christmas" was anonymously published in 1823. It's credited to Clement Clarke Moore, but some say Henry Livingston Jr. penned it. Authorship debates: the original festive drama!

Elvis Presley's "Blue Christmas" was not initially well-received by critics. Now, it's a staple of holiday playlists. Haters gonna hate, Elvis.

The 1990 film "Die Hard" is often considered a Christmas movie, igniting endless debates.

The song "Let It Snow! Let It Snow! Let It Snow!" was written by Sammy Cahn and Jule Styne during a California heatwave. Oh, the irony!

Charles Dickens whipped up "A Christmas Carol" in just six weeks. And while it was a financial gamble for him, it turns out ghosts and miserly old men were the hit combo of 1843.

"Elf" used forced perspective to make Buddy look like a giant in the North Pole scenes, rather than CGI. Old-school tricks for modern elf antics!

"Silent Night" was originally written as a poem by Joseph Mohr in 1816. It was later set to music by Franz Xaver Gruber in 1818.

In "Miracle on 34th Street," the scenes of the Macy's Thanksgiving Day Parade are of the actual parade held in 1946. Talk about real-time filming!

In "The Nutcracker," the "Dance of the Sugar Plum Fairy" is famously played with a celesta, giving it a magical twinkle.

The 1983 film "A Christmas Story" was based on semi-autobiographical stories by Jean Shepherd, who also provides the movie's narration.

Eartha Kitt's song "Santa Baby" was a tongue-in-cheek look at the post-war consumer boom. The song still rings true, given our modern consumer culture.

"Little Women" by Louisa May Alcott starts and ends with a Christmas scene. It's like a literary Christmas sandwich.

Nat King Cole's "The Christmas Song" was written during a sweltering summer, in an effort to "stay cool by thinking cool."

T.S. Eliot's poem "The Journey of the Magi" is often read at Christmas despite its rather bleak tone. Christmas isn't all tinsel and sugarplums!

The Muppet version of "A Christmas Carol" surprisingly stays true to much of Dickens' original text, despite its puppet-filled antics. Turns out, Muppets can have a serious side too!

"Deck the Halls" dates back to the 16th century, making it one of the oldest Christmas carols still sung today.

When "Gremlins" was released in 1984, it was one of the films that led to the creation of the PG-13 rating due to its blend of horror and comedy.

The Grinch was inspired by Dr. Seuss himself. He created the character after looking in the mirror on December 26th and feeling a little "grinchy."

The movie "Love Actually" originally had 14 different storylines. It was hard enough keeping up with the 10 they chose!

"Hark! The Herald Angels Sing" was written by Charles Wesley, the brother of John Wesley, founder of the Methodist church. Holy sibling rivalry, Batman!

The 1951 adaptation of "A Christmas Carol," known as "Scrooge" in the UK, is considered by many to be the definitive film version.

Judy Garland's song "Have Yourself a Merry Little Christmas" from the movie "Meet Me in St. Louis" had to be rewritten because the original lyrics were too depressing.

"Feliz Navidad" by José Feliciano was one of the earliest Christmas songs to include both English and Spanish lyrics. ¡Felices fiestas!

The beloved Rankin/Bass TV special "Rudolph the Red-Nosed Reindeer" from 1964 used a stop-motion animation technique called "Animagic," which involved miniature sets and figures.

O. Henry's 'The Gift of the Magi' from 1905 is a Christmas tale with one of literature's most iconic plot twists. Forget Christmas surprises, this story wrote the book on it!

Wham!'s "Last Christmas" has been covered over 500 times in various languages. It's the song that keeps on giving—whether you like it or not.

Despite the chaos behind the scenes of 'Bad Santa,' including multiple directors and editors, the dark comedy has secured its spot as a holiday cult classic. Even bad Santas have their day!

The 1947 song "Here Comes Santa Claus" was inspired by the annual Hollywood Christmas Parade in California. A star-studded origin, indeed!

In the 1982 animated film 'The Snowman', the hauntingly beautiful 'Walking in the Air' was actually sung by choirboy Peter Auty. Aled Jones popularized it later with his version.

Dr. Seuss was initially resistant to turning "How the Grinch Stole Christmas" into an animated film until he heard Boris Karloff would be narrating. Who could say no to that voice?

In the iconic "Christmas Vacation" film, Clark Griswold's dream of having a perfect Christmas lights display was thwarted by a single faulty bulb. We've all been there, right?

Recorded in 1984, 'Do They Know It's Christmas?' by Band Aid was a charity initiative to combat the Ethiopian famine. Spearheaded by Bob Geldof and Midge Ure, it brought together a constellation of British and Irish pop stars. The single raised over £8 million for famine relief. Talk about music with a mission!

The character of Tiny Tim in "A Christmas Carol" is believed to have been inspired by the real-life disabled nephew of Dickens.

The movie "Elf" features a cameo by Peter Billingsley, who played Ralphie in "A Christmas Story." It's like a surprise gift within a gift!

Irving Berlin won an Oscar for "White Christmas," the song he initially wrote for the movie "Holiday Inn" in 1942. The man was a holiday hit machine!

"I Saw Mommy Kissing Santa Claus" was condemned by the Roman Catholic Church in Boston when it was first released. They lifted the ban after meeting with the songwriter.

While many cozy up with tales of Santa and snow, J.D. Salinger set his short story 'A Perfect Day for Bananafish' around Christmas without a hint of festive cheer. Because who says Christmas stories have to actually be about Christmas?

The meticulous attention to detail in 'Arthur Christmas' meant animators added 25 individual frames for just one second of the film. Talk about a festive labor of love!

Jim Carrey had to undergo CIA torture-resistance training to endure the makeup process for "How the Grinch Stole Christmas." Talk about commitment to the role!

The perennial favorite "Rockin' Around the Christmas Tree" by Brenda Lee was recorded when she was only 13 years old. Prodigy, much?

The "Twelve Days of Christmas" song was first published in England in 1780, without music, as a chant or rhyme.

"Grandma Got Run Over by a Reindeer," the novelty Christmas song, was penned by Randy Brooks in 1978. Not everyone found it funny, but it still gets airplay every year.

The TV special "Rudolph the Red-Nosed Reindeer" features Burl Ives as the narrator and the voice of Sam the Snowman. Ives was a famous folk singer at the time.

Edward Pola and George Wyle, who wrote "It's the Most Wonderful Time of the Year," also wrote the theme song for "Gilligan's Island." Talk about range!

"The Best Christmas Pageant Ever" was a book before it was turned into a TV movie in 1983. The book, written by Barbara Robinson in 1971, still graces school reading lists today.

The famous phrase "Yes, Virginia, there is a Santa Claus" comes from an 1897 editorial in The New York Sun, written in response to a letter from an 8-year-old girl named Virginia O'Hanlon.

"Home Alone" and "Home Alone 2" were both written by John Hughes, the iconic '80s filmmaker behind hits like "The Breakfast Club" and "Ferris Bueller's Day Off."

In 1944, Donald Yetter Gardner penned the hit "All I Want for Christmas Is My Two Front Teeth" after hearing his second graders' lisped wishes.

The Grinch's green hue was chosen by animator Chuck Jones. Dr. Seuss had never specified the character's color.

Frank Loesser originally wrote "Baby, It's Cold Outside" as a private song for him and his wife, Lynn Garland, to perform at their housewarming party. They sang the duet together as a humorous way to announce to their guests that it was time for them to leave.

"Miracle on 34th Street" was released in May because studio executives thought more people went to the movies during the summer. They even had to play down the Christmas angle in promotional material.

The Christmas-themed romantic comedy "The Holiday" starring Cameron Diaz and Kate Winslet was a commercial success, grossing over $200 million worldwide.

In 2017, Disney released 'Olaf's Frozen Adventure,' a 21-minute holiday-themed featurette set in the world of 'Frozen.' In it, Olaf the snowman goes on a mission to find a holiday tradition for sisters Elsa and Anna, who realize they don't have any. This heartwarming tale was intended to highlight the importance of family and holiday traditions. The featurette originally premiered in theaters before Pixar's 'Coco' but was later broadcast on ABC as a standalone television special.

Alvin and the Chipmunks' "The Chipmunk Song (Christmas Don't Be Late)" won three Grammy Awards in 1958. A squeaky triumph!

The 2003 movie "Love Actually" had a Christmas-themed sequel in 2017, albeit a short one, made for charity as part of the Red Nose Day fundraising efforts.

When 'Jingle Bell Rock' by Bobby Helms hit the airwaves in 1957, it was considered quite revolutionary. Merging holiday sentiment with the upbeat tempos of the burgeoning rock 'n roll movement was a bold move. And it paid off—within just a few weeks of its late-year release, jukeboxes across America were playing it on repeat. Today, it's hard to imagine the holiday season without this pioneering crossover.

Catchy tunes have staying power! The 1942 movie 'Holiday Inn' gave us the iconic song 'White Christmas.' Flash forward 74 years, and boom! Broadway was jamming to it in a 2016 musical. Timeless or just ageless?

Mel Tormé co-wrote "The Christmas Song" ("Chestnuts Roasting on an Open Fire") during a blistering hot summer as a way to "stay cool."

Robert Zemeckis, who directed "The Polar Express," also directed the "Back to the Future" trilogy. Time travel and a magical train? Typecasting!

The character Ebenezer Scrooge from "A Christmas Carol" has been portrayed by actors ranging from Patrick Stewart to Jim Carrey to Michael Caine (in Muppet form!).

The TV special "A Charlie Brown Christmas" was so popular that it led to more than 50 further Peanuts specials and four feature films.

The Trans-Siberian Orchestra's Christmas album has been among the top 10 selling Christmas albums in the U.S. since it was released in 1996.

Did you know that while "Sleigh Ride" is now synonymous with Christmas, the song's lyrics never specifically mention the holiday? Composed by Leroy Anderson during a heatwave in July 1946, its winter-themed lyrics were added two years later by Mitchell Parish.

Clement Clarke Moore, who wrote "A Visit from St. Nicholas," was initially hesitant to publish it as he feared it would undermine his position as a professor of Oriental and Greek literature.

The movie "Scrooged" features all four acting Murray brothers – Bill, Brian Doyle-Murray, Joel Murray and John Murray. A Christmas haunting truly becomes a family affair!

Sources

Clare, Natalie. 2017. "A CHRISTMAS CAROL: Fast Facts." Cin. December 15. https://cincyplay.com/blog-single-post/cinncinati-blog/2017/12/15/a-christmas-carol-fast-facts.

Strauss, Valerie. 2021. "'Jingle Bells' - Written for Thanksgiving?" The Washington Post. WP Company. November 30. https://www.washingtonpost.com/news/answer-sheet/wp/2013/12/24/jingle-bells-written-for-thanksgiving/.

Serafino, Jason. 2022. "How 'It's a Wonderful Life' Went From Box Office Dud to Accidental Christmas Tradition." Mental Floss. Mental Floss. December 22. https://www.mentalfloss.com/article/90135/how-its-wonderful-life-went-box-office-dud-accidental-christmas-tradition.

"White Christmas (Song)." 2023. Wikipedia. Wikimedia Foundation. September 23. https://en.wikipedia.org/wiki/White_Christmas_(song).

"The History Of Rudolph The Red-Nosed Reindeer." 2015. NPR. NPR. December 25. https://www.npr.org/2015/12/25/461005670/the-history-of-rudolph-the-red-nosed-reindeer.

MacDonald, Ruth (1988). Dr. Seuss. Twayne Publishers. ISBN 0-8057-7524-2. Magazine, Smithsonian. 2015. "The 'Charlie Brown Christmas' Special Was the Flop That Wasn't." Smithsonian.Com. Smithsonian Institution. December 9. https://www.smithsonianmag.com/history/charlie-brown-christmas-special-history-television-classic-cbs-180957490/.

Hardiman, Jess. 2017. "Buzz's Girlfriend In 'Home Alone' Is Actually A Boy In Costume." LADbible. LADbible. December 5. https://www.ladbible.com/entertainment/film-and-tv-the-secret-behind-buzzs-girlfriend-in-home-alone-20171205.

Farinholt, Lenny. 2019. "The Polar Express and the Era of Motion Capture." Byrd Theatre. December 20. https://byrdtheatre.org/news/2019/12/the-polar-express-and-the-era-of-motion-capture/.

"Frosty the Snowman." 2023. Wikipedia. Wikimedia Foundation. August 29. https://en.wikipedia.org/wiki/Frosty_the_Snowman.

Scott, Rachael. 2021. "How World War II Shaped 'It's a Wonderful Life.'" CNN. Cable News Network. December 25. https://edition.cnn.com/2021/12/25/entertainment/its-a-wonderful-life-jimmy-stewart-world-war-ii/index.html.

"Exhibit: Revisiting 'A Visit from St. Nicholas.'" 2023. New York State Library. Accessed September 28. https://www.nysl.nysed.gov/collections/stnick. "When Elvis Presley Sang 'Blue Christmas' for the Last Time." 2019. Country Thang Daily. November 2. https://www.countrythangdaily.com/presley-blue-christmas/.

"How a California Heat Wave Inspired a Christmas Hit." 2023. Spectrum News NY1. Accessed September 28. https://ny1.com/nyc/all-boroughs/weather/2022/12/07/the-history-behind-the-holiday-song--let-it-snow--.

"Ten Things To Know About Charles Dickens' A Christmas Carol." 2023. National Endowment for the Arts. Accessed September 28. https://www.arts.gov/stories/blog/2020/ten-things-know-about-charles-dickens-christmas-carol.

"How They Shot Elf with Forced Perspective." 2020. Austin Kleon. December 28. https://austinkleon.com/2020/12/28/how-they-shot-elf-with-forced-perspective/.

"Silent Night." 2023. Wikipedia. Wikimedia Foundation. September 21. https://en.wikipedia.org/wiki/Silent_Night.

Busch, Jenna. 2022. "Filming In An Actual Macy's Thanksgiving Parade Meant Long Nights For The Miracle On 34th Street Cast." /Film. /Film. December 1. https://www.slashfilm.com/1122423/filming-in-an-actual-macys-thanksgiving-parade-meant-long-nights-for-the-miracle-on-34th-street-cast.

"The Nutcracker." 2023. Wikipedia. Wikimedia Foundation. September 27. https://en.wikipedia.org/wiki/The_Nutcracker.

Clarendon, Dan. 2023. "A 'Christmas Story' Story: Did You Know the Movie Already Has Its Own Cinematic Universe?" TV Insider. Accessed September 28. https://www.tvinsider.com/1068729/a-christmas-story-backstory-jean-shepherd-tv-movies.

"Santa Baby, One Thing We Really Need ... Some Christmas Commercialism." 2022. Consumer Goods Technology. December 14. https://consumer-goods.com/santa-baby-one-thing-we-really-need-some-christmas-commercialism.

Elsie. 2023. "The Little Women Guide to a Simple, Joy-Filled Christmas." Tea and Ink Society. https://teaandinksociety.com/little-women-christmas/. "The Christmas Song." 2023. Nat King Cole - The Christmas Song Lyrics | Lyrics.Com. Accessed September 28. https://www.lyrics.com/lyric/15635/Nat+King+Cole/The+Christmas+Song.

"Journey of the Magi - T. S. Eliot." 2022. Poetry Archive. September 21. https://poetryarchive.org/poem/journey-magi/.

"The Muppet Christmas Carol." 2023. Wikipedia. Wikimedia Foundation. September 16. https://en.wikipedia.org/wiki/The_Muppet_Christmas_Carol. "Deck the Halls." 2023. Wikipedia. Wikimedia Foundation. September 26. https://en.wikipedia.org/wiki/Deck_the_Halls.

Horn, Shawn Van. 2023. "We Have 'Gremlins' & 'Temple of Doom' To Thank for the PG-13 Rating." Collider. May 17. https://collider.com/gremlins-indiana-jones-temple-of-doom-pg-13-rating/.

Daley, Katerina. 2018. "20 Details Behind The Making Of Love Actually." ScreenRant. December 13. https://screenrant.com/love-actually-behind-the-scenes-details-trivia/.

Longanecker12/22/16, By: Josh. 2017. "Story Behind: Hark The Herald Angels Sing - Christmas Carols." JRC. December 20. https://jamesriver.church/blog/story-behind-hark-herald-angels-sing.

Gass, Zach. 2022. "A Christmas Carol: Ranking 18 Versions From Least To Most Accurate To The Book." ScreenRant. December 17. https://screenrant.com/christmas-carol-versions-ranked-least-most-accurate-book.

"The Dark Truth behind Original 'Have Yourself A Merry Little Christmas' Lyrics." 2020. 7NEWS. December 24. https://7news.com.au/entertainment/music/have-yourself-a-merry-little-christmas-original-lyrics-trend-c-1827292.

Magazine, Smithsonian. 2019. "The Magical Animation of 'Rudolph the Red-Nosed Reindeer.'" Smithsonian.Com. Smithsonian Institution. December 23. https://www.smithsonianmag.com/innovation/magical-animation-rudolph-red-nosed-reindeer-180973841/.

Shmoop Editorial Team. 2008. "The Gift of the Magi What's Up With the Ending?" Shmoop. Shmoop University. November 11. https://www.shmoop.com/study-guides/literature/gift-of-the-magi/analysis/ending.

"ASCAP Announces Top 25 Holiday Songs of the Decade". ASCAP. November 23, 2009. Retrieved September 28, 2023.

Gilchrist, Todd. 2012. "Bad Santa (Director's Cut)." IGN. IGN. May 17. https://www.ign.com/articles/2006/10/10/bad-santa-directors-cut.

"'Here Comes Santa Claus' Song Inspired by Hollywood Christmas Parade." 2014. ABC7 Los Angeles. November 29. https://abc7.com/hollywood-christmas-parade-november-30-stevie-wonder-grand-marshal-gene-autry-here-comes-santa-claus-down-lane-song/415311/.

"Yorkshire-Born Tenor Peter Auty Looks Back on Singing Walking in the Air in The Snowman." 2022. Yorkshire Post. December 21. https://www.yorkshire-post.co.uk/whats-on/arts-and-entertainment/peter-auty-remembers-singing-walking-in-the-air-40-years-on-3958320.

"How the Grinch Stole Christmas! (TV Special)." 2023. Wikipedia. Wikimedia Foundation. September 11. https://en.wikipedia.org/wiki/How_the_Grinch_Stole_Christmas!_(TV_special).

"National Lampoon's Christmas Vacation." 2023. Wikipedia. Wikimedia Foundation. September 28. https://en.wikipedia.org/wiki/National_Lampoon%27s_Christmas_Vacation.

Curtis-Horsfall, Thomas. 2021. "The Story of... 'Do They Know It's Christmas?' by Band Aid." Smooth. Smooth. December 9. https://www.smoothradio.com/features/the-story-of/do-they-know-its-christmas-band-aid-lyrics-artists/.

Nelson, Roxanne. 2002. "The Case of Tiny Tim." The Washington Post. WP Company. December 24. https://www.washingtonpost.com/archive/lifestyle/wellness/2002/12/24/the-case-of-tiny-tim/778d452c-16d2-48c9-99df-60c54d84c42f/.

Sharf, Zack. 2018. "The Internet Is Just Discovering Ralphie From 'A Christmas Story' Stars in 'Elf,' and Minds Are Blown." IndieWire. IndieWire. December 9. https://www.indiewire.com/features/general/ralphie-a-christmas-story-stars-in-elf-internet-discovers-peter-billingsley-1202026706/.

"White Christmas." 2023. Wikipedia. Wikimedia Foundation. September 23. https://en.wikipedia.org/wiki/White_Christmas_(song).

"I Saw Mommy Kissing Santa Claus." 2023. Wikipedia. Wikimedia Foundation. May 14. https://en.wikipedia.org/wiki/I_Saw_Mommy_Kissing_Santa_Claus.

"A Perfect Day for Bananafish." 2023. Wikipedia. Wikimedia Foundation. September 26. https://en.wikipedia.org/wiki/A_Perfect_Day_for_Bananafish.

"Arthur Christmas." 2023. Wikipedia. Wikimedia Foundation. September 10. https://en.wikipedia.org/wiki/Arthur_Christmas.

Spyscape. 2023. "How the CIA Trained Jim Carrey to Endure The Grinch 'Torture.'" SPYSCAPE. Accessed September 28. https://spyscape.com/article/jim-carrey-trained-with-a-cia-torture-expert-to-play-grinch.

"Rockin' Around the Christmas Tree." 2023. Wikipedia. Wikimedia Foundation. September 25. https://en.wikipedia.org/wiki/Rockin%27_Around_the_Christmas_Tree.

09488049085, Edgar Ebro. 2023. The Twelve Days of Christmas (1780). Accessed September 28. https://edgarebrochristmassongs.blogspot.com/2016/12/the-twelve-days-of-christmas-1780.html.

"The Story Behind 'Grandma Got Run Over By A Reindeer.'" 2015. CBS News. CBS Interactive. December 25. https://www.cbsnews.com/texas/news/interview-with-grandma-got-run-over-song-writer/.

"Burl Ives." 2023. Wikipedia. Wikimedia Foundation. September 27. https://en.wikipedia.org/wiki/Burl_Ives.

"George Wyle." 2023. Wikipedia. Wikimedia Foundation. March 7. https://en.wikipedia.org/wiki/George_Wyle.

"The Best Christmas Pageant Ever." 2023. Concord Theatricals. Accessed September 28. https://www.concordtheatricals.com/p/2282/the-best-christmas-pageant-ever.

"Research Guides: Yes Virginia, There Is a Santa Claus: Topics in Chronicling America: Introduction." 2023. Introduction - Yes Virginia, There Is a Santa Claus: Topics in Chronicling America - Research Guides at Library of Congress. Accessed September 28. https://guides.loc.gov/chronicling-america-yes-virginia.

IMDb. 2023. "John Hughes | Writer, Producer, Director." IMDb. IMDb.com. Accessed September 28. https://www.imdb.com/name/nm0000455/.

Walters, Jamie Ann. 2018. "The History Behind the Tune 'All I Want For Christmas Is My Two Front Teeth.'" Greenvilletheatre. greenvilletheatre. December 12. https://www.greenvilletheatre.org/single-post/2018/12/12/the-history-behind-the-tune-all-i-want-for-christmas-is-my-two-front-teeth.

Jones, Brian Jay, Sally Beaudette, Jeanne Wolf, and Donald Liebenson. 2019. "How Dr. Seuss Stole Christmas." The Saturday Evening Post. December 16. https://www.saturdayeveningpost.com/2019/12/how-doctor-seuss-stole-christmas.

Andersen, Neil. 2022. "Baby It's Cold Outside: The Saga of a Song." Association for Media Literacy. Association for Media Literacy. August 15. https://aml.ca/baby-its-cold-outside/.

"Miracle on 34th Street Movie Locations." 2023. On Location Tours. Accessed September 28. https://onlocationtours.com/locations/miracle-on-34th-street.

"The Holiday." 2023. Wikipedia. Wikimedia Foundation. September 9. https://en.wikipedia.org/wiki/The_Holiday.

"Olaf's Frozen Adventure." 2023. Wikipedia. Wikimedia Foundation. September 17. https://en.wikipedia.org/wiki/Olaf%27s_Frozen_Adventure.

Cox, Stephen. 2018. "'The Chipmunk Song' Turns 60: Secrets of a Holiday Novelty Smash." The Hollywood Reporter. The Hollywood Reporter. December 21. https://www.hollywoodreporter.com/news/music-news/chipmunk-song-turns-60-secrets-a-holiday-classic-1169762/.

"Red Nose Day Actually." 2023. Wikipedia. Wikimedia Foundation. September 11. https://en.wikipedia.org/wiki/Red_Nose_Day_Actually.

McIntyre, Hugh. 2019. "'Jingle Bell Rock' Sets An Important Record For The Man Behind The Christmas Classic." Forbes. Forbes Magazine. https://www.forbes.com/sites/hughmcintyre/2019/01/02/jingle-bell-rock-sets-this-important-record-for-the-man-behind-the-christmas-classic/.

"Holiday Inn (1942)." 1970. FilmAffinity. https://www.filmaffinity.com/en/film270796.html.

"The Weird Origins of Some Classic Holiday Tunes." 2023. Sudbury.Com. Accessed September 28. https://www.sudbury.com/local-news/the-weird-origins-of-some-classic-holiday-tunes-496609.

IMDb. 2023. "Robert Zemeckis | Producer, Writer, Director." IMDb. IMDb.com. Accessed September 28. https://www.imdb.com/name/nm0000709/.

"Ebenezer Scrooge." 2023. Wikipedia. Wikimedia Foundation. September 21. https://en.wikipedia.org/wiki/Ebenezer_Scrooge.

"A Charlie Brown Christmas." 2023. Wikipedia. Wikimedia Foundation. August 28. https://en.wikipedia.org/wiki/A_Charlie_Brown_Christmas.

"Christmas Eve and Other Stories." 2023. Wikipedia. Wikimedia Foundation. August 19. https://en.wikipedia.org/wiki/Christmas_Eve_and_Other_Stories.

Literawiki, Contributors to. 2023. "A Visit from St. Nicholas." Literawiki. Fandom, Inc. Accessed September 28. https://literature.fandom.com/wiki/A_Visit_from_St._Nicholas.

"Sleigh Ride." 2023. Wikipedia. Wikimedia Foundation. September 15. https://en.wikipedia.org/wiki/Sleigh_Ride.

Wood, Jennifer M. 2021. "22 Fun Facts About Scrooged </Em>." Mental Floss. Mental Floss. December 18. https://www.mentalfloss.com/article/71730/22-fun-facts-about-scrooged.

Iconic Characters and Symbols

Ho! Ho! Ho! From jolly old Saint Nick to twinkling stars atop trees, the symbols and characters of Christmas are as integral to the holiday as the presents beneath the tree. But where did Santa get his signature look? And how did a simple fir tree become the centerpiece of festive celebrations?

In this chapter, we'll trace back the origins of our favorite holiday mascots and the meaning behind iconic decorations. Prepare to uncover tales of reindeer games, twinkling lights, and festive folklore that have shaped our modern-day yuletide.

Santa Claus evolved from St. Nicholas, a 4th-century Christian bishop from modern-day Turkey known for his generosity. In Dutch, he was called "Sinterklaas," which phonetically morphed into "Santa Claus" in English.

St. Nicholas is not only the patron saint of children but also of sailors, merchants, and even repentant thieves. A man of many hats—just like Santa!

The Coca-Cola Company played a major role in popularizing the modern image of Santa Claus, featuring a jolly, red-suited, and rotund figure in their ads starting in 1931. Ah, the magic of capitalism!

The Christmas tree tradition originated in 16th-century Germany and was popularized in England by Queen Victoria and Prince Albert in the 19th century.

The star on top of the Christmas tree symbolizes the Star of Bethlehem, which guided the Wise Men to the baby Jesus. GPS, biblical style!

Elves in the modern sense were popularized through a 1823 poem titled "A Visit from St. Nicholas" (more commonly known as "The Night Before Christmas"). Thanks to this, Santa's workforce expanded dramatically!

In Scandinavian folklore, the "Yule Goat" was initially responsible for delivering presents before Santa Claus stole his gig. Sorry, Yule Goat. You're just not as marketable.

The first depiction of Mrs. Claus dates back to the 1851 poem "A Christmas Legend" by James Rees. She finally got some recognition for keeping the North Pole running smoothly!

During the times of the Ancient Greeks, couples would smooch under the mistletoe at weddings, believing it boosted fertility. So, it wasn't just a sneaky way to snag a kiss at holiday parties!

Santa's red and green attire wasn't just a festive fashion choice! According to color psychologists, red represents warmth, and green signifies renewal. Talk about dressing for success!

✲✲✲

Christmas stockings likely originated from the Dutch custom of leaving shoes filled with food for St. Nicholas' donkeys. The Saint would then replace the food with small gifts. Essentially, the first gift exchange program!

✲✲✲

The nutcracker doll became a symbol of good luck in German folklore. Breaking a tough nut was seen as overcoming adversity. Now it mostly symbolizes the start of Christmas shopping season!

The Christmas wreath is said to symbolize eternal life and the victory of the everlasting over the temporal. Deep stuff for a bunch of leaves, huh?

The poinsettia, native to Mexico, became a Christmas symbol due to its bright red leaves resembling the Star of Bethlehem. The red leaves are actually modified leaves called "bracts," not flowers!

In Catalonia, it's tradition to hunt for the "Caganer" in nativity scenes. This little figurine, often shown in the act of defecation, adds a dose of humor to the festivities. Where's Waldo, holiday edition!

Fruitcake, dense with preserved fruits and nuts, has its origins in ancient Roman recipes. Legend has it, some of the ones we get today might just be from back then!

✦✦✦

Frosty the Snowman came to life not just with a magical hat but also in the 1950 song by Walter "Jack" Rollins and Steve Nelson. He was created to capitalize on the success of "Rudolph the Red-Nosed Reindeer."

✦✦✦

Ebenezer Scrooge's first name comes from a Hebrew word that means "Stone of Help." A far cry from his initial "Bah, Humbug!" attitude.

The "X" in "Xmas" isn't actually taking the "Christ" out of "Christmas." The X is a Greek abbreviation for Christ. So, it's still keeping the reason for the season.

The Krampus, a horned figure in Germanic folklore, is basically the anti-Santa who punishes naughty children. Think of him as Santa's bad cop.

In Australia, Santa's sleigh is often said to be pulled by kangaroos. Can you imagine Rudolph with a pouch?

The concept of hanging ornaments on a Christmas tree dates back to the 16th century. Early ornaments were often fruits, nuts, and other simple objects.

Christmas lights were popularized by Edward H. Johnson, an associate of Thomas Edison, who lit up his Christmas tree with 80 red, white, and blue bulbs in 1882. Oh say, can you see the electric bill?

The Three Wise Men, also known as the Magi, are commonly named Melchior, Caspar, and Balthazar, although the Bible doesn't actually name them.

Christmas bells ring to herald Jesus' birth and to shoo away evil spirits. It's like a heavenly doorbell with built-in ghost repellent!

In some Eastern Orthodox traditions, there are 12 dishes served for Christmas Eve dinner to represent the 12 apostles. So if you're feeling apostle-sized hunger, you're in the right place!

The custom of sending Christmas cards began in Britain in 1843, started by Sir Henry Cole and John Horsley. The first card, with a print-run of 1000, had three panels and cost a shilling—basically the Victorian version of a Hallmark moment.

The Christmas spider is a popular legend in Ukraine, where a spider spun a web that turned into silver and gold when touched by sunlight. Now, Christmas spider ornaments are considered good luck.

✶✶✶

The Island of Misfit Toys in the Rudolph tale is where broken and unwanted toys go, but did you know it was a late addition to the story in 1964? Before that, Rudolph was just a one-reindeer show!

✶✶✶

Contrary to popular belief, the Bible doesn't actually specify that there were only three Wise Men. The number three comes from the gifts they brought: gold, frankincense, and myrrh.

Did you know that the red-nosed reindeer was almost named "Rollo" or "Reginald"? Thankfully, Rudolph just has a better ring to it!

"O Tannenbaum," the German carol that inspired "O Christmas Tree," originally wasn't a Christmas song at all. It was a folk song about the evergreen quality of the fir tree.

The modern concept of Santa's workshop was popularized by the 1821 poem "The Children's Friend," where Santeclaus (as it was spelled) was described as having a workshop where he built toys.

Jingle bells were actually used on sleighs and carriages to announce their approach in snowy weather, which is a bit more practical than just a catchy song lyric.

✸✸✸

The Christmas pickle is a mostly American tradition with purported German origins. A pickle ornament is hidden on the tree, and the first to find it gets an extra gift or good luck for the new year. Talk about being in a pickle!

✸✸✸

Originally from medieval Europe, eggnog had a strong ale base. The ale preserved it, eggs and milk made it festive, and let's be honest, a little booze helped everyone get into the holiday spirit!

In Spain and some other Catholic countries, the main gift-giving day is January 6th, Epiphany, in honor of the Three Wise Men. Smart—they can snag all their gifts in the Boxing Day sales!

The Yule log tradition hails from Scandinavia and represents the Old Norse god Thor. Sorry, Marvel fans, no hammers involved.

The first gingerbread men were reportedly baked by Queen Elizabeth I, who wanted them to resemble visiting guests. I guess it's the most delicious form of flattery?

In Greece, children go caroling with a triangle, drum, or even a small boat to represent the country's maritime history. They don't usually accept cookies; they prefer small gifts or money.

The first department store to feature a Santa Claus was the J. W. Parkinson's store in Philadelphia in 1841. The gig was a hit, and other stores quickly jumped on the ho-ho-ho wagon.

The word "carol" originally meant to dance in a circle, which is how the first Christmas carols were performed—danced in a circle around the Christmas tree.

The red Poinsettia is not a flower; it's a leaf. Yep, those red things are leaves, and the actual flower is the tiny yellow middle. Nature's festive deception!

✸✸✸

Peppermint has been a holiday favorite flavor since the 1600s, but did you know it's not just tasty but also a natural muscle relaxant? Perfect for those stressful family get-togethers.

✸✸✸

The term "Boxing Day," celebrated the day after Christmas, originally referred to the distribution of boxes of money or gifts to the less fortunate.

Gingerbread houses were popularized by the Brothers Grimm in their fairy tale, "Hansel and Gretel." Who knew they were such architects?!

✿✿✿

The tradition of Christmas pantomimes is particularly strong in the UK, featuring slapstick comedy and cross-dressing lead males known as "pantomime dames."

✿✿✿

The symbology behind the "Christingle" involves an orange representing the world, a candle representing Jesus's light, and fruits and nuts symbolizing God's creations. It's like a science project, but holier.

"Saint Nicholas." 2023. Wikipedia. Wikimedia Foundation. September 28. https://en.wikipedia.org/wiki/Saint_Nicholas.

Redacción. 2023. "Sobre Cómo Coca-Cola No Se Inventó a Santa Claus." Reason Why. Accessed September 28. https://www.reasonwhy.es/actualidad/santa-claus-invento-coca-cola-publicidad-navidad.

"How Queen Victoria Introduced America to the Christmas Tree: Blog." 2023. Findmypast. Accessed September 28. https://www.findmypast.co.uk/blog/history/queen-victoria-christmas-tree.

Davidspell. 2022. "Why Is There a Star on Top of My Christmas Tree?" DavidSpell.Com. December 2. https://davidspell.com/why-is-there-a-star-on-top-of-my-christmas-tree/.

Pappas, Stephanie. 2013. "Elf on a Shelf: The Strange History of Santa's Little Helpers." LiveScience. Purch. December 18. https://www.livescience.com/42051-history-of-elves.html.

"Visit." 2023. Carnegie Museum of Natural History. Accessed September 28. https://carnegiemnh.org/the-yule-goat/.

Horowitz, Kate. 2016. "The Secret History of Mrs. Claus." Mental Floss. Mental Floss. December 21. https://www.mentalfloss.com/article/90113/secret-history-mrs-claus.

Norton, Lily. 2022. "Pucker Up! Why Do People Kiss Under the Mistletoe?" LiveScience. Purch. September 27. https://www.livescience.com/32901-why-we-kiss-under-mistletoe.html.

"What Makes Red the Color of Christmas?" 2023. Psychology Today. Sussex Publishers. Accessed September 28. https://www.psychologytoday.com/intl/blog/color-psychology/202012/what-makes-red-the-color-christmas.

"The History of the Christmas Stocking." 2018. Creative Homemaking. November 23. https://creativehomemaking.com/holidays/christmas/christmas-stocking-history/.

Perron, Austin. 2022. "What Is the Story Behind the German Nutcracker?" Frankenmuth Clock & German Gift Co. Frankenmuth Clock & German Gift Co. April 26. https://frankenmuthclock.com/blogs/news/what-is-the-story-behind-the-german-nutcracker.

Moon, Kat. 2018. "Where Did Christmas Wreaths Originate? History of Tradition." Time. Time. December 21. https://time.com/5482144/christmas-wreath-origins.

"The Poinsettia: Jesus' Life Story in a Plant." 2019. The United Methodist Church. December 19. https://www.umc.org/en/content/the-poinsettia-tells-jesus-life-story.

"Caganer." 2023. Wikipedia. Wikimedia Foundation. September 16. https://en.wikipedia.org/wiki/Caganer.

"Fruitcake Has Always Been Around Since Its Origins in Ancient Rome." 2018. Palm Springs Life. November 30. https://www.palmspringslife.com/fruitcake-history.

Kovalchik, Kara. 2017. "8 Jolly Happy Facts About Frosty the Snowman." Mental Floss. Mental Floss. December 22. https://www.mentalfloss.com/article/72865/8-jolly-happy-facts-about-frosty-snowman.

Nino. 2016. "The Ebenezer Syndrome: Beverly Hills Film Festival: Official Site." Beverly Hills Film Festival | Official Site. December 23. https://beverly-hillsfilmfestival.com/ebenezer-syndrome.

Ambrosino, Brandon. 2014. "The X in Xmas Literally Means Christ. Here's the History behind It." Vox. Vox. December 14. https://www.vox.com/2014/12/14/7374401/jesus-xmas-christmas.

"Krampus." 2023. Wikipedia. Wikimedia Foundation. September 19. https://en.wikipedia.org/wiki/Krampus.

"Australian Christmas Tradition: Singing Six White Boomers!" 2023. Little Passports. February 27. https://www.littlepassports.com/blog/world-holidays/australia-christmas-tradition/.

Culturetrip. 2023. "A Brief History Of The Christmas Ornament." Culture Trip. September 28. https://theculturetrip.com/europe/germany/articles/a-brief-history-of-the-christmas-ornament-3.

"Edward Hibberd Johnson." 2022. Wikipedia. Wikimedia Foundation. November 22. https://en.wikipedia.org/wiki/Edward_Hibberd_Johnson.

Grandchamp, Greg. 2021. "Do We Know the Three Wise Men's Names in the Bible?" Christianity.Com. Christianity.com. December 15. https://www.christianity.com/wiki/holidays/do-we-know-the-three-wise-mens-names-in-the-bible.html.

"Christmas Bell History." 2023. Christmascarnivals. Accessed September 28. http://www.christmascarnivals.com/christmas-history/christmas-bell-history.html.

"Twelve-Dish Christmas Eve Supper." 2023. Wikipedia. Wikimedia Foundation. March 28. https://en.wikipedia.org/wiki/Twelve-dish_Christmas_Eve_supper.

"The First Christmas Card." 2023. The Postal Museum. https://www.postal-museum.org/collections/first-christmas-card.

"Legend of the Christmas Spider." 2023. Wikipedia. Wikimedia Foundation. July 9. https://en.wikipedia.org/wiki/Legend_of_the_Christmas_Spider.

Cronin, Brian. 2017. "Were the Misfit Toys Not Originally Saved When Rudolph the Red-Nosed Reindeer First Aired?" HuffPost. HuffPost. December 7. https://www.huffpost.com/entry/were-the-misfit-toys-not_b_8685668.

Waxman, Olivia B. 2020. "Here's What History Can Tell Us About the Magi." Time. Time. December 29. https://time.com/5923009/three-kings-wisemen-history-magi-bible.

"O Tannenbaum." 2023. Wikipedia. Wikimedia Foundation. September 13. https://en.wikipedia.org/wiki/O_Tannenbaum.

"The Children's Friend." 2023. Craig Hosterman. Accessed September 28. http://www.santaswhiskers.com/the-children-s-friend.html.

"Jingle Bell." 2023. Wikipedia. Wikimedia Foundation. May 3. https://en.wikipedia.org/wiki/Jingle_bell.

"Christmas Pickle." 2023. Wikipedia. Wikimedia Foundation. May 24. https://en.wikipedia.org/wiki/Christmas_pickle.

"Eggnog." 2023. Wikipedia. Wikimedia Foundation. August 3. https://en.wikipedia.org/wiki/Eggnog.

Allen, Lisa. 2020. "Castle Object of the Month: Yule Log Painting." Hever Castle. December 1. https://www.hevercastle.co.uk/news/castle-object-month-yule-log-painting.

Tabb, Michael. 2017. "England's 'Virgin Queen' Invented Gingerbread Men to Represent Her Suitors." Quartz. Quartz. December 20. https://qz.com/quartzy/1161865/gingerbread-men-were-invented-by-queen-elizabeth-i-to-represent-her-suiters.

Team, GCT, Athens Bureau, and Guest Contributor. 2020. "Christmas Eve Tradition - Greek Kalanda (VIDEO)." Greek City Times. December 24. https://greekcitytimes.com/2020/12/24/christmas-eve-greek-kalanda.

University, Central Michigan. 2004. "The History of Santa Claus Merchandising." Newswise. Newswise. November 3. https://www.newswise.com/articles/the-history-of-santa-claus-merchandising.

2023. The Origin of Carol Singing. | Achievements. Accessed September 28. https://www.family-history.co.uk/news/2015/12/the-origin-of-carol-singing.

"Poinsettia." 2023. Wikipedia. Wikimedia Foundation. August 17. https://en.wikipedia.org/wiki/Poinsettia.

"The Best Natural Muscle Relaxers and How to Use Them." 2023. Medical News Today. MediLexicon International. Accessed September 28. https://www.medicalnewstoday.com/articles/323393.

"Boxing Day." 2023. Encyclopædia Britannica. Encyclopædia Britannica, inc. September 25. https://www.britannica.com/topic/Boxing-Day.

"Hansel and Gretel." 2023. Wikipedia. Wikimedia Foundation. September 16. https://en.wikipedia.org/wiki/Hansel_and_Gretel.

"Befana." 2023. Wikipedia. Wikimedia Foundation. June 19. https://es.wikipedia.org/wiki/Befana.

"The History Of The Christingle." 2023. The History Of The Christingle | Out of the Ark Blog | Out of the Ark Music. Accessed September 27. https://www.outoftheark.co.uk/blog/the-history-of-the-christingle/.

Winter
Flora & Fauna

Beneath the winter's blanket of snow and amidst the festive jingles, nature presents its own holiday spectacle. From the deep green of mistletoe to the flight of reindeer across Arctic skies, winter's flora and fauna play a starring role in our Christmas narratives. But what secrets do these plants and creatures hold? How did holly find its way into our homes, and what makes reindeer suited for their icy habitats? So, lace up your winter boots and grab a cozy scarf; we're setting off on a yuletide nature trail!

Ever wonder why we kiss under mistletoe? The Druids believed mistletoe had magical powers, but let's face it, it's more about sneaking a kiss from your crush, isn't it?

🌲🌲🌲

Mistletoe is actually a parasite that attaches itself to trees to get nutrients. So, the tradition of stealing a kiss under it is, well, a little less appealing now.

🌲🌲🌲

Mistletoe has white berries, while holly has red ones. But don't mix them up! Mistletoe berries are toxic to pets. No puppy kisses under this plant!

🌲🌲🌲

Did you know that holly leaves' sharp edges are thought to represent Christ's crown of thorns and the red berries his blood? Holy holly symbolism!

Holly is dioecious, meaning it has separate male and female plants. Only the female plants produce those iconic red berries.

🌲🌲🌲

Ever think of the first person to put a tree indoors for Christmas? While 16th-century Germans get the credit, the tradition took its sweet time reaching U.S. shores. Up until the 19th-century, Americans thought an indoor tree was... tree-ly strange.

🌲🌲🌲

1930 saw the birth of the artificial Christmas tree, courtesy of the Addis Brush Company. Using their toilet brush machinery, they just dyed the bristles green. So, in a way, the first fake tree was pretty... 'flush' with innovation!

Norway spruces are the most commonly used Christmas tree in Europe. These trees can grow up to 215 feet! Talk about a tree-mendous holiday!

🎄🎄🎄

In Canada and the U.S., over 40 million real Christmas trees are sold each year. That's a lot of chopping!

🎄🎄🎄

In 2021, Canada shipped over 2.4 million fresh Christmas trees, and 97.2% of them took a trip south to the United States. I guess the neighbors just couldn't resist that Canadian evergreen charm, eh?

Turkeys and geese have been a part of festive feasts for centuries. The domestication of turkeys began around 800 B.C. by indigenous peoples in Mexico, while geese were domesticated in Egypt over 3,000 years ago. Their transition from farmyard to festive table has cemented their status as holiday favorites.

🎄🎄🎄

During the Victorian era, Christmas cards sometimes featured images of dead robins. This may seem morbid by today's standards, but it was symbolic of the fragility of life and a reminder of the cycle of the seasons. Robins, with their bright red breasts, were often associated with the festive season and were seen as messengers of the spirit world, bridging the gap between life and death.

Reindeer are native to Arctic regions and are well-suited for it. Their noses warm the air they breathe before it reaches their lungs. Talk about built-in central heating!

🎄🎄🎄

Male reindeer shed their antlers in early December, while females keep theirs through the winter. So, technically, Santa's reindeer would likely be female!

🎄🎄🎄

The North American reindeer is called a Caribou. They're the same species, just different names depending on their location. No word on whether they're jealous of their flying cousins.

Penguins must have lost their GPS! While these cold-weather-loving birds often appear on Christmas cards, penguins don't actually live in the northern hemisphere (asides a lone species on the Galapagos Islands).

🎄🎄🎄

According to the National Christmas Tree Association, it takes an average of seven years to grow a Christmas tree to marketable size. That's a lot of TLC (Tree Loving Care)!

🎄🎄🎄

Oregon doesn't just excel in hipster vibes and coffee; it's also the reigning champ in Christmas tree production. With the fir tree proudly displayed on its state flag and an impressive 4 million Christmas trees produced annually (making up 30% of the U.S. total), it's safe to say Oregon takes its evergreens seriously.

Discarded Christmas trees have been used to make sand and soil erosion barriers. Even after the holidays, they're still doing good!

🎄🎄🎄

Artificial Christmas trees have been around since the 19th century and were initially made of goose feathers. A bit of a fowl choice?

🎄🎄🎄

Research shows that the Christmas and New Year holiday period is associated with a 25% increase in daily waste generated by an average American household. Time to think about eco-friendly gift wrapping!

The ecological footprint of a real Christmas tree
is 16 kg of CO_2. In contrast, an artificial tree has a
footprint of approximately 40 kg of CO_2. So choose
wisely!

🎄🎄🎄

Every year, one ton of recycled Christmas paper
saves 17 trees, 380 gallons of oil, and 4,000 kilowatts
of energy. Wrap your head around that!

🎄🎄🎄

In the U.K., it's estimated that 160,000 tonnes of
Christmas trees get thrown away after the holidays.
That's a lot of wasted wood!

🎄🎄🎄

A snowflake can be made up of as many as 200
ice crystals, all sticking together. Just a tiny
masterpiece from Mother Nature, no big deal!

Did you know that polar bears have black skin underneath their fur to help them absorb and retain heat? Bet you thought they were white through and through!

☘ ☘ ☘

The Arctic springtail, a tiny insect living in the Arctic, produces a natural antifreeze compound to survive extremely cold temperatures. Winter's chill doesn't faze this little critter!

☘ ☘ ☘

Cinnamon, one of the popular spices during Christmas, comes from the inner bark of cinnamon trees. And here you thought it was just for making things tasty!

Squirrels are a significant problem for Christmas tree growers. They like to cut off the growing tips of the tree for food. Naughty, not nice!

🎄 🎄 🎄

Ever thought about the weight of snow? An inch of snow over an acre can be anywhere from 1,300 to 5,400 gallons of water, depending on its fluffiness. Talk about a heavy blanket!

🎄 🎄 🎄

The pine needles of a Christmas tree, especially from the Eastern White Pine can be brewed to make a vitamin C-rich tea. Be careful though, some can also be toxic!

Christmas Island, a territory of Australia, is more famous for its red crab migration than for any Yuletide festivities.

🎄🎄🎄

The ribbon-like parasite that mistletoe uses to attach itself to its host tree is called a haustorium. Sounds more like a rejected Hogwarts house, doesn't it?

🎄🎄🎄

The phrase "to deck the halls" originated from the old English expression for decorating a large public room or hall.

Penguins can dive up to 1,500 feet deep and hold their breath for more than 20 minutes. That's a lot of time spent fishing for Christmas dinner!

🎄🎄🎄

One of the original uses of frankincense was as a mosquito repellent. Gold, frankincense, and no mosquito bites—a true Christmas miracle!

🎄🎄🎄

In Mexico, where Poinsettias hail from, they don't just grow... they skyrocket! We're talking 10-15 feet tall. Who knew they had such lofty ambitions?

The Christmas fern got its name because its fronds stay green throughout the year, including Christmas! That's some dedicated holiday spirit.

🎄🎄🎄

Many Christmas tree farmers use chickens to control pests naturally. Call it the peck-tacular method of organic farming.

🎄🎄🎄

There are around 15,000 Christmas tree farms in the U.S., employing over 100,000 people. That's a lot of elves... err, employees.

Festive plants like mistletoe, ivy, holly, and poinsettias can be harmful to pets. Keep your fur babies safe this holiday season!

🌲🌲🌲

Reindeer are the only mammal that can see ultraviolet light, which helps them see in the polar darkness. Rudolph's nose isn't the only one with superpowers!

🌲🌲🌲

According to the National Turkey Federation, over 22 million turkeys are consumed each Christmas in the U.S. Talk about being stuffed!

Contrary to popular belief, poinsettias aren't highly toxic to humans. But eating them can still cause mild irritation, so it's best to stick to cookies.

🎄 🎄 🎄

In Arizona, one can find the world's largest tumbleweed Christmas tree. Because nothing says Christmas like a giant ball of dry, prickly brush!

Boucher, Carolyn. Norfolk Botanical Garden. 2020. "Mystical Mistletoe." Norfolk Botanical Garden. Norfolk Botanical Garden. December 15. https://norfolkbotanicalgarden.org/mystical-mistletoe.

"Mistletoe Poisoning: MedlinePlus Medical Encyclopedia." 2023. MedlinePlus. U.S. National Library of Medicine. Accessed September 28. https://medlineplus.gov/ency/article/002883.html.

Bjornstad, Grace. 2022. "The Holly Plant's Role in the Symbolism of Christmas." Mission Viejo. February 16. https://www.missionviejoflorist.com/blog/the-holly-plants-role-in-the-symbolism-of-christmas/.

Stacey. 2023. "Did You Know? Hollies Are Dioecious." Mid. Accessed September 28. https://midatlanticgardening.com/did-you-know-hollies-are-dioecious/.

"Christmas Tree Facts." 2023. Christmas Tree Facts - Christmas Trees and More - University of Illinois Extension. Accessed September 28. https://web.extension.illinois.edu/trees/facts.cfm.

"Norway Spruce: National Christmas Tree Association." 2019. National Christmas Tree Association | Every Christmas Needs a Real Tree. August 1. https://realchristmastrees.org/education/tree-varieties/norway-spruce/.

"Quick Tree Facts: National Christmas Tree Association." 2019. National Christmas Tree Association | Every Christmas Needs a Real Tree. July 29. https://realchristmastrees.org/education/quick-tree-facts/.

BirdNote. 2023. "The Long, Surprising Journey of the Domestic Wild Turkey." Audubon. February 21. https://www.audubon.org/news/the-long-surprising-journey-domestic-wild-turkey.

Meier, Allison. 2022. "Why Are There Dead Birds on Victorian Christmas Cards?" Hyperallergic. July 13. https://hyperallergic.com/344920/why-are-there-dead-birds-on-victorian-xmas-cards/.

Medicine, Center for Veterinary. 2023. "Fun Facts about Reindeer and Caribou." U.S. Food and Drug Administration. FDA. Accessed September 28. https://www.fda.gov/animal-veterinary/animal-health-literacy/fun-facts-about-reindeer-and-caribou.

Osc. 2021. "Cool Reindeer Facts You Didn't Know." Orlando Science Center. December 7. https://www.osc.org/reindeer-facts.

Medicine, Center for Veterinary. 2023. "Fun Facts about Reindeer and Caribou." U.S. Food and Drug Administration. FDA. Accessed September 28. https://www.fda.gov/animal-veterinary/animal-health-literacy/fun-facts-about-reindeer-and-caribou.

"Why Are There No Penguins in the Arctic?" 2023. Discover Wildlife. Accessed September 28. https://www.discoverwildlife.com/animal-facts/birds/why-are-there-no-penguins-in-the-arctic.

Cole, Kay Dee. 2022. "Which States Rank Highest for Christmas Tree Production?: Clarity." Clarity Wealth Development. December 5. https://www.claritywealthdevelopment.com/which-states-rank-the-highest-for-christmas-tree-production.

Anonymous. 2016. "Using Christmas Trees to Trap Sand: Connecticut Beaches and Dunes: A Hazard Guide for Coastal Property Owners." Connecticut Beaches and Dunes A Hazard Guide for Coastal Property Owners. July 22. https://beachduneguide.uconn.edu/is-the-beach-is-eroding/using-christmas-trees-for-erosion-control/.

"German Feather Trees." 2023. HERMANN FARM. Accessed September 28. https://hermannfarm.org/feather-trees.

"Data Point: Have Yourself a Merry Little (Waste-Free) Christmas." 2023. The Economist. The Economist Newspaper. Accessed September 28. https://impact.economist.com/sustainability/circular-economies/data-point-have-yourself-a-merry-little-waste-free-christmas.

L, Jennifer. 2023. "Christmas Tree Carbon Emissions: The Real vs. Fake Breakdown." Carbon Credits. March 7. https://carboncredits.com/christmas-tree-carbon-emissions-the-real-vs-fake-breakdown.

"Impact." 2023. Greenii Inc. Accessed September 28. https://greenii.ca/pages/impact.

"How Much Waste Does the Festive Season Create?" 2023. How Much Waste Does the Festive Season Create? - PHS Wastekit. Accessed September 28. https://phswastekit.co.uk/blog/posts/20-11-2018/how-much-waste-does-the-festive-season-create.

Education, UCAR Center for Science. 2023. "SkySci for Kids." What Are Snowflakes? | Center for Science Education. Accessed September 28. https://scied.ucar.edu/kids/snowstorms-blizzards/snowflakes-activity.

"Why Do Polar Bears Have White Fur? And Nine Other Polar Bear Facts." 2023. WWF. World Wildlife Fund. Accessed September 28. https://www.worldwildlife.org/stories/why-do-polar-bears-have-white-fur-and-nine-other-polar-bear-facts.

Clark, Melody S, Michael AS Thorne, Jelena Purać, Gavin Burns, Guy Hillyard, Željko D Popović, Gordana Grubor-Lajšić, and M Roger Worland. 2009. BMC Genomics 10 (1): 328. doi:10.1186/1471-2164-10-328.

"Christmas Tree Pests and Weeds." 2023. Wikipedia. Wikimedia Foundation. September 12. https://en.wikipedia.org/wiki/Christmas_tree_pests_and_weeds.

"Rain and Precipitation Completed." 2023. Rain and Precipitation | U.S. Geological Survey. Accessed September 28. https://www.usgs.gov/special-topics/water-science-school/science/rain-and-precipitation.

"10 Reasons You Should Be Drinking Pine Needle Tea." 2023. Forest Holidays. Accessed September 28. https://www.forestholidays.co.uk/forestipedia/10-reasons-you-should-be-drinking-pine-needle-tea/.

"Red Crab Migration." 2023. Australian Government. Accessed September 28. https://parksaustralia.gov.au/christmas/discover/highlights/red-crab-migration/.

"Haustorium." 2023. Encyclopædia Britannica. Encyclopædia Britannica, inc. Accessed September 28. https://www.britannica.com/science/haustorium.

"How Penguins & Seals Survive Deep Dives." 2023. NSF. Accessed September 28. https://new.nsf.gov/news/how-penguins-seals-survive-deep-dives.

Metayi, Mervat H, Shimaa S Abd El-Naby, Noha A El-Habal, Heba H Fahmy, Mona S Abdou, Baber Ali, Khaled H Abdel-Rheim, and Ahmed Abdel-Megeed. 2022. "Omani Frankincense Nanoemulsion Formulation Efficacy and Its Latent Effects on Biological Aspects of the Spiny Bollworm Earias Insulana (Boisd.)." Frontiers in Physiology. U.S. National Library of Medicine. October 6. https://www.ncbi.nlm.nih.gov/pmc/articles/PMC9583008/.

Martin, Tovah. 2022. "Poinsettia Care Guide & Growing Tips - Garden Design." GardenDesign.Com. Garden Design Magazine. November 30. https://www.gardendesign.com/flowers/poinsettias.html.

"Polystichum Acrostichoides." 2023. Purveyor of Native Plant Life. Accessed September 28. https://www.possibilityplace.com/our-plants/polystichum-acrostichoides.

"Regenerative Farming." 2023. Isham Family Farm. Accessed September 28. https://www.ishamfamilyfarm.com/organic-farming.

"Which Christmas Plants Are Poisonous to Dogs?" 2023. The Kennel Club. Accessed September 28. https://www.thekennelclub.org.uk/health-and-dog-care/health/health-and-care/a-z-of-health-and-care-issues/which-christ-mas-plants-are-poisonous-to-dogs/.

Dominy, Nathaniel J. 2015. Frontiers for Young Minds 3 (December). doi:10.3389/frym.2015.00018.

"Turkey Facts." 2023. Turkey Facts - Turkey for Holidays - University of Il-linois Extension. Accessed September 28. https://web.extension.illinois.edu/turkey/turkey_facts.cfm.

"Are Poinsettias Poisonous?" 2023. Poison Control. Accessed September 28. https://www.poison.org/articles/poinsettias.

22, Nov., and Communications and Public Affairs. 2022. "Where Did Chan-dler Get Its Tumbleweed Tree?" City of Chandler. November 23. https://www.chandleraz.gov/blog/where-did-chandler-get-its-tumbleweed-tree.

"Deck the Halls." 2023. GRAMMARIST. September 4. https://grammarist.com/phrase/deck-the-halls/.

Christmas in Pop Culture

From the iconic lines of "Home Alone" to the heartwarming melodies of "White Christmas," pop culture has been instrumental in shaping how we perceive and celebrate the festive season.

Dive into this chapter to explore the myriad ways Christmas has been immortalized in movies, music, literature, and television.

In 2021, 21 years after its original airing, the 'Holiday Armadillo' episode of 'Friends' had a pop culture resurgence, proving that armadillos, like fine wine, only get better with age!

♥♥♥

In 2022, King Charles delivered his first Royal Christmas Message, stepping into a role his mother, Queen Elizabeth II, had held since 1952.

♥♥♥

Macaulay Culkin reprised his "Home Alone" role for a Google Assistant commercial in 2018. 28 years later, and he's still messing with burglars!

Mariah Carey's "All I Want for Christmas Is You" broke three Guinness World Records, including most-streamed track on Spotify in 24 hours. Talk about a Christmas miracle!

In the 2019 TV special, "The Kacey Musgraves Christmas Show," Kacey Musgraves and Lana Del Rey sing "I'll Be Home for Christmas." Because nothing says home like a country-pop crossover.

Stephen Colbert's 2008 "A Colbert Christmas" won a Grammy for Best Comedy Album. It's the gift that keeps on giving...laughs.

Justin Bieber's "Under the Mistletoe" album went platinum just a month after its release in 2011. Beliebers really know how to jingle those bells.

♥ ♥ ♥

Elvis Presley's "Blue Christmas" was originally recorded in 1948 by Doye O'Dell. But let's face it, nothing says Christmas like The King's swiveling hips.

♥ ♥ ♥

Dolly Parton and Kenny Rogers' 1984 Christmas album "Once Upon a Christmas" went double platinum. Because you can't spell Christmas without C-O-U-N-T-R-Y.

The first "Saturday Night Live" Christmas sketch aired on December 20, 1975. Who needs cookies and milk when you've got comedy?

Vince Guaraldi's jazz soundtrack for "A Charlie Brown Christmas" was groundbreaking at the time for an animated special. Songs like "Linus and Lucy" and "Christmas Time Is Here" have since become classic holiday standards. Yet, initially, the jazzy score was another reason network executives were unsure about the special. Who'd have thought jazz and cartoons would make such a delightful combo?

Taylor Swift wrote "Christmas Tree Farm" based on her childhood experience working on a Christmas tree farm. No "Bad Blood" there, just good tidings.

"Die Hard" is a Christmas movie. Fight me.

♥ ♥ ♥

The Hallmark Channel produces about 40 new Christmas movies every year. Because you can never have too much holiday cheese.

♥ ♥ ♥

Ariana Grande's "Santa Tell Me" has over 800 million Spotify streams. That's a Grande-sized serving of Christmas spirit!

♥ ♥ ♥

Oprah's 'Favorite Things' list, running since 1996, has given everything from UGGs to Kindles the sales 'Oomph!' of approval. It's the gift that keeps on giving... to retailers!

The 1977 duet of 'Little Drummer Boy' paired rock icon David Bowie with the classic crooner Bing Crosby, a combination as unexpected as pineapple on pizza. Yet, with Bowie's added 'Peace on Earth' counterpoint, it turned into a holiday hit!

The Simpsons' first-ever episode was a Christmas special. "Simpsons Roasting on an Open Fire" debuted on December 17, 1989.

Lea Michele, who starred in "Glee," released a Christmas album called "Christmas in the City" in 2019. It's a Gleeful holiday, indeed!

In 2018, Friends of Portsmouth (USA) set the record for the most people caroling with 1,880 participants. Portsmouth, Ohio suddenly became the unofficial capital of 'Jingle Bells' that day!

♥♥♥

Ellen DeGeneres hosted "Ellen's 12 Days of Giveaways" for 20 years, before the final one in 2021.

♥♥♥

Zooey Deschanel, known for her role in "Elf," is one-half of the duo She & Him, which has released two Christmas albums. That's what I call "elf-tastic"!

♥♥♥

In 2012, Gangnam Style's Psy released a Christmas remix, because nothing says Yuletide like "Oppan Christmas Style."

The first-ever "Rudolph the Red-Nosed Reindeer" TV special aired in 1964. Ah, the age before reindeer became influencers.

♥♥♥

Meghan Markle and Prince Harry's first Christmas card featured a never-before-seen photo from their wedding. A royal way to spread holiday cheer!

♥♥♥

Whitney Houston's "One Wish: The Holiday Album" went gold. Because when Whitney sings, all our wishes come true.

♥♥♥

Michael Bublé's "Christmas" was the best-selling album of 2011 in Australia, making Bublé the first non-Australian artist to have Australia's best-selling album for two years (his album "Crazy Love" was the best seller in 2009).

In "The Polar Express," Tom Hanks voiced six different characters: Hero Boy, Father, Conductor, Hobo, Scrooge, Santa Claus. Talk about wearing many (Santa) hats!

♥♥♥

Kelly Clarkson's "Wrapped in Red" album is certified platinum. We've been "Stronger" since she came into our lives.

♥♥♥

Snoop Dogg's 2008 Christmas album, "Snoop Dogg Presents Christmas in tha Dogg House," diverged from traditional holiday tunes. It featured collaborations with artists like Soopafly, Kurupt, and J. Black. With tracks like "Look Out" and "A Pimp's Christmas Song," it's clear that Snoop delivered holiday vibes with his unique West Coast twist. Makes you wonder if Santa rides lowriders in Long Beach!

Mariah Carey's 'All I Want for Christmas Is You' has reportedly earned her around US$2.5 million annually. By 2016, she'd raked in a cool US$60 million. With that kind of cash, she could probably buy the North Pole and give Santa a raise!

The Beatles, ever the trendsetters, released special Christmas records for their fan club from 1963 to 1969. Because nothing says 'Beatlemania' like John, Paul, George, and Ringo wishing you a 'fab' festive season!

James Corden's Christmas Carpool Karaoke featured celebrities from Adele to Lady Gaga. Now, that's what I call a star-studded sleigh ride!

Disney chose suspense over sales in 2019 by withholding Baby Yoda toy designs until "The Mandalorian" debuted. This Jedi-level storytelling move cost them an estimated $2.7 million in missed holiday merchandise sales. With 90,000 Amazon searches in one month for Baby Yoda toys, it's clear fans felt a disturbance in the merchandising force.

The Grinch who stole Christmas? Jim Carrey spent 92 days in makeup to get into character for the 2000 film. Talk about dedication!

The iconic holiday Coca-Cola commercials featuring polar bears first debuted in 1993. Cheers to fuzzy Christmas cheer!

Disney's "The Santa Clause" trilogy starring Tim Allen has grossed over $470 million worldwide. Santa's sleigh isn't the only thing soaring.

A Reddit Secret Santa exchange made headlines when a user got Bill Gates as their Secret Santa. Who needs Santa when you have a billionaire?

All of the royalties from the sales of Bob Dylan's 'Christmas in the Heart' go directly to the charities Feeding America in the USA, Crisis in the UK, and the World Food Programme. So, not only did Dylan surprise fans with a holiday album, but he also made sure the spirit of giving was truly embedded in it!

Britney Spears' song "My Only Wish (This Year)" has been a holiday hit since its release in 2000, and is particularly popular in Germany. Oops!... She did it again.

♥ ♥ ♥

Will Ferrell turned down $29 million to star in an "Elf" sequel. Apparently, even elves have their price.

♥ ♥ ♥

Did you know that while 'Last Christmas' by Wham! is one of the best-selling singles of all time in the UK, it didn't reach the coveted number one spot until 2021? It was kept from the top by Band Aid's 'Do They Know It's Christmas?' in 1984. Talk about tough holiday competition!

Netflix's "A Christmas Prince" was so popular that it spawned two sequels. Talk about a crowning achievement!

J.K. Rowling has written multiple Harry Potter Christmas scenes, including the unforgettable Yule Ball. Not just a magical Hogwarts event, Yule Balls have since become real-world celebrations, with fans hosting them globally. No Muggles allowed... unless they're good dancers!

The Kardashians' annual Christmas card is more than just a festive greeting. Over the years, it has become a pop culture event, with elaborate themes, glamorous outfits, and occasional hints dropped about family dynamics. We're still waiting on ours...

"The Nightmare Before Christmas" is so versatile it can be watched on Halloween and Christmas. Double-duty holiday spirit!

♥♥♥

Adam Sandler's "The Chanukah Song" became an instant holiday classic when it debuted on SNL in 1994. Eight crazy nights, one awesome song.

♥♥♥

"Black Mirror's" episode "White Christmas" is a holiday special for the dystopian crowd. Joy to the (future) world?

♥♥♥

Ludacris narrated and produced an animated Netflix show called "Ludacris Saves Christmas." That's Ludacris-tmas for you!

In 2020, Dolly Parton released her first holiday album in 30 years, "A Holly Dolly Christmas." Notably, it includes collaborations with family members and other stars like Miley Cyrus, Michael Bublé, and Jimmy Fallon. Dolly once remarked that the pandemic gave her the time to work on the album, turning a challenging period into a time of festive creativity.

♥♥♥

Brenda Lee was just 13 years old when she recorded "Rockin' Around the Christmas Tree." It was released in 1958 but only gained significant popularity after Lee became a star. Now, it's hard to imagine the holiday season without it, showcasing how hits sometimes need time to find their audience.

Nick Offerman's "Yule Log" video has gained a cult following. It's 45 minutes of him silently drinking whiskey by a fire.

♥ ♥ ♥

The Muppets and John Denver released a Christmas album in 1979. Muppet-tastic!

♥ ♥ ♥

The Christmas episode of "The Office," "Christmas Party," aired in 2005 and is still a fan favorite. In fact, it was nominated for two Primetime Emmy awards. "That's what she said"—Santa, probably.

♥ ♥ ♥

Seth Rogen's "The Night Before" aimed to be the "Superbad" of Christmas movies. Naughty or nice, you decide.

"Frosty the Snowman" was inspired by the 1950 song, but became a TV classic in 1969. Frosty never looked so good for his age.

The "South Park" Christmas Special, "Mr. Hankey, the Christmas Poo," was a surprise hit in 1997. The idea of a talking piece of feces might seem offbeat, but it was their unique way of addressing the controversies surrounding the commercialization and secularization of Christmas.

♥ ♥ ♥

Billy Mack's character in "Love Actually" was supposedly inspired by two famous British rock stars, Mick Jagger and Rod Stewart. Who knew love was all around us?

"Peanuts" creator Charles Schulz was hesitant to include a Bible verse in "A Charlie Brown Christmas." Thankfully, he took the leap of faith.

♥ ♥ ♥

KFC is so popular in Japan during Christmas that orders are placed months in advance. The tradition began in the 1970s when KFC Japan began the "Kurisumasu ni wa kentakkii!" (Kentucky for Christmas!) marketing campaign. Nothing says "Merry Christmas" like a bucket of fried chicken!

♥ ♥ ♥

Ryan Reynolds narrated a humorous behind-the-scenes look at his famous "ugly Christmas sweater" prank. The prank took place during a holiday gathering with fellow actors Hugh Jackman and Jake Gyllenhaal. They told Reynolds it was a sweater party, but when he showed up in his festive garb, he was the only one in theme. Only Ryan could make ugly look so good.

Spotify's data-driven approach to curating playlists reveals interesting patterns. For instance, during the 2017 holiday season, data showed that listeners began streaming holiday music in large numbers right after Halloween, with the trend peaking on Christmas Eve.

♥♥♥

In the UK, a competition for the "Christmas Number One" single heats up every year. This tradition dates back to the 1950s. Over the years, a range of songs, both festive and not, have achieved the Christmas number one spot. It's a fiercely contested accolade and has even seen grassroots campaigns beat major artists to the top spot. The charts are making a list and checking it twice!

♥♥♥

The 2015 film "Krampus" became a dark horse holiday hit, grossing over $61 million worldwide. Ho ho horror!

Destiny's Child's "8 Days of Christmas" album gave us a modern take on a classic tune. On the 8th day of Christmas, my true love gave to me... Beyoncé!

♥ ♥ ♥

"Fairytale of New York" by The Pogues is the most-played Christmas song of the 21st century in the UK. No fairytale, just facts!

♥ ♥ ♥

Boyz II Men's "Let it Snow" featuring Brian McKnight is a Christmas R&B classic. Snow never sounded so smooth.

♥ ♥ ♥

Zooey Deschanel's iconic shower duet in "Elf" wasn't originally scripted but was a last-minute addition due to her singing chops! Fun fact: Will Ferrell surprised her with his undercover singing talent, proving elves have hidden skills.

Sources

Tolsky, Molly. 2021. "21 Years After Its 'Friends' Debut, the Holiday Armadillo Is Having a Moment." Kveller. November 12. https://www.kveller.com/21-years-after-its-friends-debut-the-holiday-armadillo-is-having-a-moment/. O'Kane, Caitlin. 2018. "Macaulay Culkin Is 'Home Alone' Again in New Ad."

CBS News. CBS Interactive. December 19. https://www.cbsnews.com/news/google-home-alone-commercial-macaulay-culkin-is-home-alone-again-in-new-ad/.

"Mariah Carey Establece 3 Récords Mundiales Guinness." 2019. Los Angeles Times. Los Angeles Times. November 29. https://www.latimes.com/espanol/entretenimiento/articulo/2019-11-29/mariah-carey-all-i-want-for-christmas-is-you-guinness-mundial-records.

"The Kacey Musgraves Christmas Show." 2023. Wikipedia. Wikimedia Foundation. July 22. https://en.wikipedia.org/wiki/The_Kacey_Musgraves_Christmas_Show.

"A Colbert Christmas: The Greatest Gift of All!" 2023. Wikipedia. Wikimedia Foundation. July 27. https://en.wikipedia.org/wiki/A_Colbert_Christmas:_The_Greatest_Gift_of_All!

"Under the Mistletoe." 2022. Wikipedia. Wikimedia Foundation. December 31. https://en.wikipedia.org/wiki/Under_the_Mistletoe.

Heichelbech, Rose. 2021. "The Very First Recording of Blue Christmas from 1948 Was a Country Song!" Dusty Old Thing. March 4. https://dustyoldthing.com/1948-doye-odell-blue-christmas/.

"Once Upon a Christmas (Kenny Rogers and Dolly Parton Album)." 2023. Wikipedia. Wikimedia Foundation. August 23. https://en.wikipedia.org/wiki/Once_Upon_a_Christmas_(Kenny_Rogers_and_Dolly_Parton_album).

"Two Saturday Night Live Christmases: 1975 and 1976." 2011. The A.V. Club. December 10. https://www.avclub.com/two-saturday-night-live-christmases-1975-and-1976-1798228839.

"A Charlie Brown Christmas (Soundtrack)." 2023. Wikipedia. Wikimedia Foundation. September 8. https://en.wikipedia.org/wiki/A_Charlie_Brown_Christmas_(soundtrack).

O'Connor, Lauren. 2023. "TV FORMAT FUNDAMENTALS: HALLMARK CHRISTMAS MOVIES." The Writers Guild Foundation. The Writers Guild Foundation. February 11. https://www.wgfoundation.org/blog/2022/12/6/hallmark-christmas-movies.

"Santa Tell Me." 2018. Spotify. November 9. https://open.spotify.com/track/62AGBURrH2EsqA7yblCGXP.

"Oprah's Favorite Things List for 2022". https://www.bestproducts.com/lifestyle/g3434/oprahs-favorite-things/. Accessed 28 September, 2023.

"David Bowie, Bing Crosby and the Story of the Strangest Christmas Duet Ever | CBC Music Read." 2022. CBCnews. CBC/Radio Canada. December 15. https://www.cbc.ca/music/read/david-bowie-bing-crosby-and-the-story-of-the-strangest-christmas-duet-ever-1.5008343.

"Simpsons Roasting on an Open Fire." 2023. Wikipedia. Wikimedia Foundation. August 17. https://en.wikipedia.org/wiki/Simpsons_Roasting_on_an_Open_Fire.

"Christmas in the City (Album)." 2023. Wikipedia. Wikimedia Foundation. August 17. https://en.wikipedia.org/wiki/Christmas_in_the_City_(album).

"Most People Carolling (Caroling)." 2023. Guinness World Records. Accessed September 28. https://www.guinnessworldrecords.com/world-records/most-people-carolling-(caroling).

Laurenti, Andrea. 2022. "Ellen DeGeneres Warmed Our Hearts With Her Final 12 Days Of Giveaways." Advocate Channel. Advocate Channel. November 2. https://advocatechannel.com/ellen-degeneres-12-days-of-christmas.

"Zooey Deschanel." 2023. Wikipedia. Wikimedia Foundation. September 28. https://en.wikipedia.org/wiki/Zooey_Deschanel.

Rolling Stone. 2018. "Psy Brings 'Gangnam Style' to Washington." Rolling Stone. Rolling Stone. June 25. https://www.rollingstone.com/music/music-news/psy-gives-gangnam-style-a-seasonal-twist-for-christmas-in-washington-80202/.

"Rudolph the Red-Nosed Reindeer (TV Special)." 2023. Wikipedia. Wikimedia Foundation. September 27. https://en.wikipedia.org/wiki/Rudolph_the_Red-Nosed_Reindeer_(TV_special).

Barcelona, Ainhoa. 2018. "Prince Harry and Meghan Release Never-before-Seen Royal Wedding Photo for Their First Christmas Card." HELLO! HELLO! December 14. https://www.hellomagazine.com/royalty/2018121465633/prince-harry-meghan-markle-baby-bump-christmas-card/

"One Wish: The Holiday Album." 2023. Wikipedia. Wikimedia Foundation. June 20. https://en.wikipedia.org/wiki/One_Wish:_The_Holiday_Album.

"Christmas (Michael Bublé Album)." 2023. Wikipedia. Wikimedia Foundation. September 15. https://en.wikipedia.org/wiki/Christmas_(Michael_Bubl%C3%A9_album).

"The Polar Express." 2023. IMDb. IMDb.com. Accessed September 28. https://www.imdb.com/title/tt0338348/characters/nm0000158.

"Wrapped in Red." 2023. Wikipedia. Wikimedia Foundation. September 17. https://en.wikipedia.org/wiki/Wrapped_in_Red.

"Snoop Dogg Presents Christmas in Tha Dogg House." 2023. Wikipedia. Wikimedia Foundation. April 5. https://en.wikipedia.org/wiki/Snoop_Dogg_Presents_Christmas_in_tha_Dogg_House.

"All She Wants for Christmas: Mariah Carey's Festive Millions, Revealed." 2022. South China Morning Post. November 13. https://www.scmp.com/magazines/style/celebrity/article/3199329/mariah-careys-christmas-millions-revealed-all-i-want-christmas-you-still-tops-music-charts-28-years.

Runtagh, Jordan. 2020. "Beatles' Rare Fan-Club Christmas Records: A Complete Guide." Rolling Stone. Rolling Stone. December 13. https://www.rollingstone.com/music/music-lists/beatles-rare-fan-club-christmas-records-a-complete-guide-120854/.

"'All I Want for Christmas' Carpool Karaoke." 2016. YouTube. YouTube. December 15. https://www.youtube.com/watch?v=JKJExBXRorA.

ComicBook. 2023. "Disney CEO Explains Lack of Baby Yoda Merchandise for Holiday Season." Star Wars. Comicbook.com. Accessed September 29. https://comicbook.com/starwars/news/star-wars-why-cant-buy-baby-yoda-merchandise-holiday-season-2019-disney-ceo-bob-iger-explains/.

Perez, Chris. 2022. "Jim Carrey Underwent 92 Grueling Transformations While Filming How The Grinch Stole Christmas." Looper. Looper. December 20. https://www.looper.com/1143278/jim-carrey-underwent-92-grueling-transformations-while-filming-how-the-grinch-stole-christmas/.

Coca Cola Polar Bears. Coca Cola. https://www.coca-colacompany.com/about-us/history/coca-colas-polar-bears. Accessed 29 September, 2023.

"The Santa Clause (Franchise)." 2023. Wikipedia. Wikimedia Foundation. September 25. https://en.wikipedia.org/wiki/The_Santa_Clause_(franchise).

kathleen_elk. 2019. "Bill Gates Sent an 81-Pound Package to His Reddit Secret Santa-Here's What Was Inside." CNBC. CNBC. December 26. https://www.cnbc.com/2019/12/26/what-bill-gates-gave-his-2019-reddit-secret-santa.html.

Petrusich, Amanda. 2009. "Bob Dylan: Christmas in the Heart." Pitchfork. Pitchfork. October 26. https://pitchfork.com/reviews/albums/13615-christmas-in-the-heart/.

"My Only Wish (This Year)." 2023. Wikipedia. Wikimedia Foundation. September 24. https://en.wikipedia.org/wiki/My_Only_Wish_(This_Year).

Rolling Stone. 2021. "Will Ferrell Turned Down $29 Million to Star in 'Elf' Sequel." Rolling Stone. Rolling Stone. October 29. https://www.rollingstone.com/tv-movies/tv-movie-news/will-ferrell-elf-sequel-turned-down-1249976/.

Cotter, Padraig. 2022. "Why It Took 36 Years For Wham's 'Last Christmas' To Reach UK Number 1." ScreenRant. February 12. https://screenrant.com/last-christmas-wham-song-36-years-uk-number-one/.

2023. Harry Potter: A Yule Ball Celebration. Accessed September 30. https://harrypotteryuleballcelebration.com/.

Burkett, +Becky. 2022. "DEBATE SOLVED: Is 'The Nightmare Before Christmas' a Halloween Film or a Christmas Film?" Disney Dining. October 27. https://www.disneydining.com/is-the-nightmare-before-christmas-a-halloween-film-or-a-christmas-film-the-director-settles-the-debate-once-and-for-all-bb1/.

"The Chanukah Song." 2023. Wikipedia. Wikimedia Foundation. September 16. https://en.wikipedia.org/wiki/The_Chanukah_Song.

"White Christmas (Black Mirror)." 2023. Wikipedia. Wikimedia Foundation. August 5. https://en.wikipedia.org/wiki/White_Christmas_(Black_Mirror).
"Nick Offerman's 'Yule Log.'" 2015. YouTube. YouTube. December 2. https://www.youtube.com/watch?v=LS-ErOKpO4E.

"John Denver and the Muppets: A Christmas Together." 2023. Wikipedia. Wikimedia Foundation. June 10. https://en.wikipedia.org/wiki/John_Denver_and_the_Muppets:_A_Christmas_Together.

"Christmas Party (The Office)." 2023. Wikipedia. Wikimedia Foundation. September 8. https://en.wikipedia.org/wiki/Christmas_Party_(The_Office).

"The Night Before." 2015. IMDb. IMDb.com. November 20. https://www.imdb.com/title/tt3530002/.

Staff, Hollywood.com. "Love Actually Review." Tickets to Movies in Theaters, Broadway Shows, London Theatre & More | Hollywood.Com, 7 June 2014, www.hollywood.com/movies/love-actually-review-57237913. Accessed 30 Sept. 2023.

Editor, ChurchPOP. 2023. "How the Bible Almost Got 'A Charlie Brown Christmas' Canceled." ChurchPOP. ChurchPOP. May 10. https://www.churchpop.com/how-the-bible-almost-got-a-charlie-brown-christmas-canceled/.

"Mr. Hankey, the Christmas Poo." 2023. Wikipedia. Wikimedia Foundation. July 16. https://en.wikipedia.org/wiki/Mr._Hankey,_the_Christmas_Poo.

Betts, Jennifer. 2023. "Frosty the Snowman: The Story in All Iterations." LoveToKnow. LoveToKnow. May 3. https://www.lovetoknow.com/celebrations/christmas/frosty-snowman.

Beauchamp, Dan. 2021. "Japan's Kentucky Christmas Tradition." Danny With Love. Danny With Love. December 25. https://www.dannywithlove.com/blog/japans-kentucky-christmas-tradition.

And elika. 2019. "After Being Pranked Into Wearing An Ugly Sweater Last Year, Ryan Reynolds Uses It To Give Back To Kids In Need." Bored Panda.

Bored Panda. December 23. https://www.boredpanda.com/ryan-reynolds-ugly-sweater-returns-hugh-jackman-sickkids.

Abby.kramer@groupsjr.com. 2018. "Is It Too Early for Christmas Music?" Spotify. November 28. https://newsroom.spotify.com/2018-11-05/is-it-too-early-for-christmas-music-2/.

"Krampus." 2015. IMDb. IMDb.com. December 4. https://www.imdb.com/title/tt3850590/.

"8 Days of Christmas." 2023. Wikipedia. Wikimedia Foundation. August 13. https://en.wikipedia.org/wiki/8_Days_of_Christmas.

"Fairytale of New York." 2023. Wikipedia. Wikimedia Foundation. July 26. https://en.wikipedia.org/wiki/Fairytale_of_New_York.

"'Elf' Star Zooey Deschanel Reveals the Story behind the 'Baby It's Cold Outside' Scene." EW.Com. Accessed October 1. https://ew.com/movies/elf-zooey-deschanel-baby-its-cold-outside-scene/.

Feasting & Festivities

The heart of Christmas often beats loudest at the dinner table. From roast turkey to figgy pudding, festive foods are as integral to the celebration as twinkling lights and wrapped presents. In this chapter, we'll journey through the rich tapestry of holiday feasts and festivities, exploring both time-honored traditions and innovative new ways people come together in culinary celebration.

Let your senses be tantalized as we delve into the flavors, aromas, and communal joys that define the season's gastronomic delights.

Americans guzzle down over 130 million pounds of eggnog every December. Its roots trace back to British aristocrats who sipped on a posh drink made of hot milk and pricey spirits. Now, it's the unofficial beverage of ugly sweater parties everywhere!

Early stollen (the popular German Christmas cake) wasn't the delightful treat we know today. In fact, due to Advent fasting rules in the 15th century, Saxony bakers were forbidden from using butter, leaving the bread hard and tasteless. It took persistent lobbying – and five popes! – before Pope Innocent VIII, in 1490, sent the now-famous "Butter-Letter" permitting butter use in stollen. The catch? Anyone wanting this buttery privilege (beyond the Prince-Elector and his household) had to pay a fee, which went towards building the Freiberg Minster.

In 1390, the English cookbook "The Forme of Cury" contained the earliest known recipe for plum pudding. "Cury" not as in curry, but as in "cookery!"

The Feast of the Seven Fishes, originally an Italian tradition, swam over to the U.S. with Italian immigrants. Why seven fishes? Maybe they were aiming for the seven sacraments or just really liked seafood. Either way, it's one fishy way Italian-Americans have reeled in the holiday spirit!

King's College in Cambridge hosts the Festival of Nine Lessons and Carols every Christmas Eve. The Christmas tradition began in 1918 and is now broadcasted to millions around the world It's like the Super Bowl for hymn enthusiasts.

The first recorded Christmas market was the Dresden Striezelmarkt in 1434. The market is named after "Striezel," which is a type of Stollen. More than just a mouthful to say, it's a mouthful of holiday goodness!

Turducken: an American holiday showstopper, bringing birds of a feather... well, inside one another. While stuffing creatures for culinary purposes dates back to ancient Rome, Chef Paul Prudhomme claims to have brought this poultry trio to the limelight in the '80s.

Mulled wine dates back to the Romans in the 2nd century. As they traveled and conquered large parts of Europe, they spread the warm goodness. Romans might not have had Santa, but they knew how to get jolly!

Joulupöytä is the traditional Finnish Christmas table, featuring unique dishes like Karelian hot pot. Nordic taste, global appeal!

The Yule Log cake, or bûche de Noël, is a French creation meant to resemble an actual Yule log. Burn calories, not wood!

Since its debut in 2003, Starbucks' Pumpkin Spice Latte, affectionately known as the PSL, has gained a cult following. Over 200 million PSLs were sold in its first decade alone! Some even joke it's the unofficial harbinger of fall, bringing with it sweater weather and leaf-peeping.

Ever heard of 'Wassail'? Hailing from Old Norse and Old English origins, it's the medieval version of 'Cheers!'—both in words and in a drink!

The sugar cookie, a Christmas staple, was created by German Protestant settlers in Nazareth, Pennsylvania. Religious freedom never tasted so sweet.

Lutefisk, a Scandinavian delicacy made of dried fish and lye, is eaten around Christmas. Not for the faint of stomach!

The biggest gingerbread house ever built was in Texas and had an interior space of 1,110 square feet. Everything is bigger in Texas, including the sweets!

Tamales are a traditional Christmas dish in several Latin American countries. Forget cookies—Santa wants tamales!

In 2013, a Christmas pudding in the UK was tagged at $38,500 due to being soaked in 200 year old Cognac, making it the 'caviar' of puddings. It's surpising considering most people would pay NOT to eat their Christmas pudding.

The Guinness World Record for the most mince pies eaten in one minute is 3. Sounds like someone saved plenty of room for seconds.

Apple cider's roots trace back to the early Romans, who then spread this deliciousness all over Europe. Ancient Rome's juiciest export!

Coquito, a Puerto Rican Christmas drink, is like the Caribbean cousin of eggnog. Made from coconut milk and rum, it's eggnog's beach-loving sibling!

Mince pies were originally filled with meat, hence the name. Modern-day "mincemeat" took a fruity turn, much to the relief of dessert lovers everywhere.

The world's largest Christmas pudding weighed 7,231 pounds (3.28 tonnes) and was made in Aughton, Lancashire, UK, in 1992. That's a lot of pudding power!

In the Czech Republic, the traditional Christmas dish, fried carp, isn't just a meal. The fish often takes a temporary residency in family bathtubs before heading to the dinner table. Sounds fishy to me!

🍪🍪🍪

Panettone, Milan's festive bread, wasn't just a Renaissance food trend—it's a love story! Legend says young Ughetto Atellani, from Milan's high society, boosted his beloved's bakery sales by jazzing up the bread with butter, sugar, and raisins. Result? A bestseller and a love story sweeter than the bread itself. Talk about baking your way to someone's heart!

🍪🍪🍪

The average American consumes around 6,500 calories on Christmas Day. Better not watch that scale!

In Spain, nougat candy known as "Turrón" is a Christmas must-have. But did you know it has Moorish roots? While both Spain's turrón and Italy's torrone likely hail from Moorish influences, the Spanish version boasts a richer almond game with at least 60% almond content—beating the Italians at their own nut game!

The White House has featured a gingerbread house every year since 1969. Talk about housing policy we can all get behind!

While bacalao is enjoyed in many countries, Portugal claims it with gusto! The Portuguese have a saying that there are 365 ways to cook bacalao, one for each day of the year. Given its ubiquity, it's no surprise that bacalao dishes are a centerpiece at many Portuguese Christmas tables.

Saffron buns are a Swedish Christmas tradition. They're bright yellow and super tasty, a little like a culinary Northern Light!

***

The world record for the largest cup of hot chocolate was set in Tampa, Florida, and held 880 gallons. Just missing a mountain of whipped cream!

***

The first Christmas stamp sparks debate! Canada's "XMAS 1898" wasn't truly festive, but many still consider it to be the first Christmas stamp. Meanwhile, British Forces in Egypt in 1935 might've beat them with a genuine Christmas spirit stamp. Who truly stamped first? The mystery unwraps!

The Christmas cracker was invented by Londoner Tom Smith in 1847. It's been sparking holiday joy—and corny jokes—ever since.

In Newfoundland, Canada, a traditional Christmas Eve dish is Jigg's dinner, which includes salt beef and boiled vegetables. Who said Christmas can't be both salty and sweet?

"Ōmisoka," or Japanese New Year's Eve, often features a bowl of toshikoshi soba noodles to say goodbye to the old year. Pasta la vista, last year!

The world record for the largest mince pie weighs in at 1.02 tonnes (2,260 lb) and was baked by Messrs L and W Radford Ltd in Burton upon Trent, UK. Measuring 20 x 5 ft, it debuted in Ashby-de-la-Zouch's 1932 shopping festival. The ingredient list boasted over a million currants and 1.5 gallons of rum! The pie was auctioned off the next day to raise funds for a local hospital.

A Christmas ale called "Samichlaus" brewed in Switzerland is one of the strongest lagers in the world at 14% alcohol by volume, and is only brewed on Saint Nicholas's Day. Santa might need a designated sleigh driver!

"Lefse," a Norwegian flatbread, often graces Christmas tables in the Midwest U.S. It's an old-world staple with new-world charm.

In France, a common Christmas Eve tradition is to have a late-night feast called "Réveillon," which literally means "awakening." One bite and you're wide awake!

Roast goose was the original British Christmas dinner before turkey dethroned it. Call it the Yule duel of fowls!

"Melomakarona" are honey-dipped cookies that are a Christmas treat in Greece. Ancient gods would surely approve!

In Poland, the Christmas Eve dinner, "Wigilia," includes "opłatek," a blessed Christmas wafer. It's like the holy grail of appetizers.

A traditional Mexican Christmas dish is "bacalao a la vizcaína," a rich stew made of salted cod, tomatoes, capers, and olives. It's a fiesta in a pot!

✶✶✶

Originating from Silesia, an historical region that now spans parts of modern-day Poland, Czech Republic, and Germany, the "Silesian Streuselkuchen" is a beloved crumb cake that's often part of Christmas celebrations in Germany. Indeed, in the world of festive confections, these crumbs truly rise to the occasion!

✶✶✶

The traditional Russian Christmas dish, "kutya," is made of grains, poppy seeds, and honey. In some traditions, a bowl of kutya is left on the table overnight to feed departed ancestors' spirits, ensuring their blessings for the home and family.

In 2017 in New York, the largest gingerbread village ever displayed contained 1,251 buildings. Looks like the gingerbread man finally found a place to settle down!

In Ethiopia, 'doro wat' is the spicy chicken stew of choice for Christmas, scooped up with injera bread. Forget utensils, the best way to taste the holidays is hands-on!

The Christmas "Pavlova" dessert, popular in Australia and New Zealand, was named after Russian ballet dancer Anna Pavlova. It's been pirouetting its way into our stomachs since!

Spiced beef is an Irish Christmas delicacy, often enjoyed cold in the days following Christmas. It's the gift that keeps on giving!

Bejgli is a Hungarian Christmas cake packed with poppy seeds or walnuts. It's the festive roll that'll make you say, 'Holy dough!'.

In the Philippines, "Noche Buena" is a grand family dinner after the Midnight Mass, featuring delicacies like "lechon" (roast pig). Midnight snack level: Expert.

In Iceland, "laufabrauð" or "leaf bread" is a traditional Christmas bread that's deep-fried and incredibly thin. It's the haute couture of bread!

Canada's "butter tarts" are a Christmas must-have. Think of them as mini pecan pies that forgot the pecans but kept all the deliciousness!

The popular Christmas dessert "Trifle," layers of sponge cake, custard, and fruit, began stealing the show in 18th-century England.

At Christmas, Venezuelans enjoy "hallacas," a mixture of beef, pork, chicken, capers, raisins, and olives wrapped in maize and boiled in banana leaves. It's basically Christmas in a leaf!

The first-ever recipe for a chocolate chip cookie, which has become a staple of Christmas cookie plates, was created by Ruth Wakefield in 1938. She was the true cookie monster!

In Greece, the cherished "Christopsomo" or "Christ's Bread" pays homage to ancient festive traditions, blending past with the present. Made from the finest ingredients, it's often adorned with dough symbols like crosses, animals, and even farm tools, reflecting family life and invoking fertility and prosperity. It's not just bread; it's a Christmas canvas of culture and devotion!

In South Africa, a common Christmas dish is "Malva pudding," a sticky, caramelized dessert. Talk about a sugar rush!

Marzipan is often shaped into fruits, pigs, or other forms for Christmas in Germany. It's like Play-Doh you can eat!

In Lithuania, "Kūčiukai" are small pastries that are dipped in poppy seed milk during Christmas Eve. Soak it all in!

The 13 desserts of Christmas, representing Jesus and the 12 apostles, is a tradition in Provence, France. A heavenly platter!

Hot buttered rum, made from butter, sugar, spices, and rum, is a classic holiday cocktail in the U.S. It's like the winter version of a piña colada!

The Sydney Fish Market, one of the world's largest fish markets, hosts an annual 36-hour trading marathon leading up to Christmas. In that time, they often sell over 100 tonnes of prawns and close to one million oysters.

In Guatemala, Christmas Eve tamales go red with "Tamales Colorados." It's like they're dressed up for the holiday party too!

***

In Colombia, "Natilla," a custard-like dessert, and "Buñuelos," cheesy fritters, are Christmas staples. It's like having two holidays in your mouth!

***

In Spain, especially in Asturias, cider is a Christmas favorite, making the holiday season as bubbly as the drink itself. Raise a glass and cider the day!

***

In 2012, the world's largest gingerbread man weighed 1,435 pounds (651 kg) and was made in Norway. Gingerbread gym, anyone?

In Brazil, a traditional Christmas food is "Chester," a type of super-chicken bred to have more meat. Because who wouldn't want more chicken?

In Sweden, "Julmust" is the Christmas drink of choice, with 45 million litres guzzled in December alone. That's 50% of the month's soft drink consumption and 75% of the yearly must sales. Talk about a festive fizz frenzy!

Sources

Scinto, Maria. 2022. "What Is Eggnog And Is It Always Alcoholic?" Mashed. Mashed. April 10. https://www.mashed.com/30967/know-taking-another-sip-eggnog/.

Bäckerei & Konditorei Gnauck UG (haftungsbeschränkt). 2023. "The History of the Christ Stollen from Dresden - Bäckerei & Konditorei Gnauck from Ottendorf-Okrilla." Bäckerei & Konditorei Gnauck. ©1919 - 2023 by Bäckerei & Konditorei Gnauck UG (haftungsbeschränkt) - Ottendorf-Okrilla | Imprint | DataProtection. Accessed October 1. https://www.stollen-online.de/dresdner-stollen/geschichte-eng.htm.

"The Forme of Cury." 2023. Wikipedia. Wikimedia Foundation. August 10. https://en.wikipedia.org/wiki/The_Forme_of_Cury.

America, The Culinary Institute of. 2022. "Christmas Eve the Italian Way Means a Feast of Seven Fishes." Tribune. San Diego Union-Tribune. December 21. https://www.sandiegouniontribune.com/lifestyle/food-and-cooking/story/2022-12-21/christmas-eve-the-italian-way-means-a-feast-of-seven-fishes.

Dresden. 2023. "Striezelmarkt Dresden." Striezelmarkt.Dresden.De. September 29. https://striezelmarkt.dresden.de/de/.

"Turducken." 2023. Wikipedia. Wikimedia Foundation. September 27. https://en.wikipedia.org/wiki/Turducken.

Lesgrappes. 2023. "Where Does Mulled Wine Come From?" Les Grappes. Accessed October 1. https://www.lesgrappes.com/en/magazine/parlons-vin/oenologie/dou-vient-le-vin-chaud.

"Joulupöytä." 2022. Wikipedia. Wikimedia Foundation. December 23. https://en.wikipedia.org/wiki/Joulup%C3%B6yt%C3%A4.

7, STPL Reference SlidellDecember, and STPL Reference Slidell. 2021. "Origins of the Yule Log Tradition." St Tammany Parish Library. December 7. https://www.sttammanylibrary.org/blogs/post/origins-of-the-yule-log-tradition

23, Heidi Peiper • August. 2023. "PSL Turns 20: The Story behind Starbucks Pumpkin Spice Latte ." Starbucks Stories. Accessed October 1. https://stories.starbucks.com/stories/2023/psl-turns-20-the-story-behind-starbucks-pumpkin-spice-latte/.

"Wassail Definition & Meaning." 2023. Merriam-Webster. Merriam-Webster. Accessed October 1. https://www.merriam-webster.com/dictionary/wassail.

"Sugar Cookie." 2023. Wikipedia. Wikimedia Foundation. September 28. https://en.wikipedia.org/wiki/Sugar_cookie.

"Lutefisk." 2023. Wikipedia. Wikimedia Foundation. September 24. https://en.wikipedia.org/wiki/Lutefisk.

"Largest Gingerbread House." 2023. Guinness World Records. Accessed October 1. https://www.guinnessworldrecords.com/world-records/largest-gingerbread-house.

Luna, Alondra. 2023. "How Tamales Became a Christmas Tradition." WOAI. Accessed October 1. https://news4sanantonio.com/news/local/how-tamales-became-a-christmas-tradition-sanantonio-texan-tradition-mesoamerican-mexican-families-hispanic-heritage.

Scoble, Roger. 2013. "The World's Most Expensive Christmas Pudding." Pursuitist. December 26. https://pursuitist.com/worlds-expensive-christmas-pudding.

"Fastest Time to Eat Three Mince Pies." 2023. Guinness World Records. Accessed October 1. https://www.guinnessworldrecords.com/world-records/fastest-time-to-eat-three-mince-pies.

"History of Cider: WSU Cider: Washington State University." 2023. WSU Cider. Accessed October 1. https://cider.wsu.edu/history-of-cider/.

Noshery, The. 2020. "Authentic Coquito Recipe: Puerto Rican Coconut Nog - The Noshery." The Noshery - a Little Something to Nosh On. October 21. https://thenoshery.com/coquito-puerto-rican-coconut-nog/.

"The History of Mince Pies." 2023. Walker's Shortbread. Accessed October 1. https://www.walkersshortbread.com/the-history-of-mince-pies/.

Life, Northern. 2023. "Northern Record Breakers • Northern Life." Northern Life Magazine. https://northernlifemagazine.co.uk/northern-record-breakers-2.

"Christmas in Europe: Carp in Your Bathtub and Other Czech Traditions." 2023. Euronews. Accessed October 1. https://www.euronews.com/2022/12/20/christmas-across-europe-carp-in-your-bathtub-and-other-czech-traditions.

Ania. 2023. "From Milan to the World: Tracing the Fascinating History of Panettone." Mediolan. July 14. https://mediolan.pl/en/history-of-panettone/.

2023. ABC News. ABC News Network. Accessed October 1. https://abcnews.go.com/Health/calories-average-american-eats-christmas/story?id=27816914.

"TURRÓN and Other Christmas Treats." 2017. MAMA ÍA. March 6. https://www.natachasanzcaballero.com/fundamentals-2/idiosyncrasies-spanish-cuisine/turron-other-christmas-treats.

"Gingerbread at the White House." 2023. WHHA (En-US). Accessed October 1. https://www.whitehousehistory.org/galleries/gingerbread-at-the-white-house. Pedroso, Célia. 2022. "The Story of Bacalhau, a Christmas Staple in Lisbon." Culinary Backstreets. December 2. https://culinarybackstreets.com/cities-category/lisbon/2022/bacalhau-2/.

North Wild Kitchen. 2020. "St. Lucia Saffron Buns (Lussekatter)." North Wild Kitchen. December 11. https://northwildkitchen.com/st-lucia-saffron-buns-lussekatter.

2023. Largest Cup of Hot Chocolate: MOSI Breaks Guinness World Record (Video). Accessed October 1. https://www.worldrecordacademy.com/food/largest_cup_of_hot_chocolate_MOSI_breaks_Guinness_world_record_213214.html.

"Christmas Stamp." 2023. Wikipedia. Wikimedia Foundation. February 19. https://en.wikipedia.org/wiki/Christmas_stamp.

"Tom Smith Crackers." 2023. Tom Smith Crackers - The History of the Christmas Cracker. Accessed October 1. https://tomsmithcrackers.co.uk.

"Jiggs Dinner." 2023. Wikipedia. Wikimedia Foundation. August 2. https://en.wikipedia.org/wiki/Jiggs_dinner.

Nami. 2023. "Toshikoshi Soba (New Year's Eve Soba Noodle Soup)." Just One Cookbook. August 3. https://www.justonecookbook.com/toshikoshi-soba/.

"Largest Mince Pie." 2023. Guinness World Records. Accessed October 1. https://www.guinnessworldrecords.com/world-records/largest-mince-pie. Rummel, Rachel. 2018. "Here Comes (14% Alcohol By Volume) Santa Claus." Atlas Obscura. Atlas Obscura. September 20. https://www.atlasobscura.com/foods/samichlaus.

"Lefse." 2023. Wikipedia. Wikimedia Foundation. September 29. https://en.wikipedia.org/wiki/Lefse#Lefse_in_the_United_States.

Alsup, Allison. 2017. "The Story Behind Réveillon, the Classic French Creole Christmas Meal." Eater New Orleans. Eater New Orleans. December 19. https://nola.eater.com/2017/12/19/16795972/reveillon-christmas-dinner-nola-tradition.

Young, Barbara. 2022. "Guidelines for Ordering Your Christmas Goose and Turkey." Good Food Ireland. November 15. https://goodfoodireland.ie/blog/ordering-your-christmas-goose-and-turkey.

Giannopoulos, Eli K. 2021. "Melomakarona Recipe (Greek Christmas Honey Cookies)." My Greek Dish. December 14. https://www.mygreekdish.com/recipe/melomakarona-greek-christmas-honey-cookies/.

"13 Polish Christmas Traditions {Wigilia Traditions in Poland}." 2023. Blog Key to Poland. Accessed October 1. https://keytopoland.com/post/13-polish-christmas-traditions-wigilia-traditions.

"Mexican Bacalao a La Vizcaina Recipe by Edson Diaz-Fuentes." 2021. The Guardian. Guardian News and Media. November 22. https://www.theguardian.com/food/2021/nov/22/mexican-bacalao-a-la-vizcaina-recipe-edson-diaz-fuentes.

Kravchuk, Natasha. 2018. "Kutia Recipe (Sweet Wheat Berry Pudding)." NatashasKitchen.Com. April 8. https://natashaskitchen.com/kutia-recipe-sweet-wheat-berry-pudding/.

"Largest Gingerbread Village." 2023. Guinness World Records. Accessed October 1. https://www.guinnessworldrecords.com/world-records/largest-gingerbread-village.

"In Ethiopia, Locals Eat a 'Doro Wat,' a Chicken Stew Served with Flat Bread. Forget the Forks and Knives, Because like with Many Ethiopian Meals, You Eat This with Your Hands." 2023. Business Insider. Accessed October 1. https://www.businessinsider.in/heres-what-people-eat-on-christmas-in-21-countries-around-the-globe/in-ethiopia-locals-eat-a-doro-wat-a-chicken-stew-served-with-flat-bread-forget-the-forks-and-knives-because-like-with-many-ethiopian-meals-you-eat-this-with-your-hands-/slideshow/56160637.cms.

"Pavlova." 2023. Encyclopædia Britannica. Encyclopædia Britannica, inc. Accessed October 1. https://www.britannica.com/topic/pavlova.

Winiarek, Magda. 2021. "Spiced Beef - A Traditional Irish Festive Treat." Good Food Ireland. July 14. https://goodfoodireland.ie/blog/spiced-beef-2/.

"Poppy Seed Roll." 2023. Wikipedia. Wikimedia Foundation. September 24. https://en.wikipedia.org/wiki/Poppy_seed_roll.

Veneracion, Connie. 2021. "How to Celebrate Christmas in the Philippines." The Spruce Eats. The Spruce Eats. May 18. https://www.thespruceeats.com/philippine-noche-buena-feast-3030319.

Eva. 2023. "Laufabrauð - Icelandic Leaf Bread." Bake. July 22. https://bake-street.com/en/laufabraud-icelandic-leaf-bread/.

Parsons, Barry C. 2022. "The Best Classic Canadian Butter Tarts - a Definite Keeper Recipe!" Rock Recipes. November 28. https://www.rockrecipes.com/best-classic-canadian-butter-tarts/.

Al-Hatlani, Alana. 2022. "What Is a Trifle?" Southern Living. Southern Living. May 31. https://www.southernliving.com/food/desserts/what-is-a-trifle.

Goya. 2023. Recipe for Venezuelan Hallacas. Accessed October 1. https://goya.es/en/recipe/recipe-for-traditional-venezuelan-hallacas.

Magazine, Yankee. 2022. "Ruth Wakefield's Original Toll House Cookies Recipe." New England. May 17. https://newengland.com/food/original-toll-house-cookies/.

Kavroulaki, Mariana. 2015. "Christopsomo." History of Greek Food. June 1. https://1historyofgreekfood.wordpress.com/category/christopsomo/.

"Malva Pudding: A South African Christmas Pudding Tradition." 2021. Vision Times. December 23. https://www.visiontimes.com/2021/12/22/malva-pudding-christmas-tradition.html.

lithuanianintheusa, Paskelbė. 2019. "Kūčiukai (Lithuanian Christmas Eve Special Cookies) / Kūčiukai." Lithuanian in the USA. https://lithuanianintheusa.com/2016/12/22/kuciukaikuciukai-lithuanian-christmas-eve-special-cookies/.

"Thirteen Desserts." 2023. Wikipedia. Wikimedia Foundation. July 6. https://en.wikipedia.org/wiki/Thirteen_desserts.

Graham, Colleen. 2023. "This Warming Hot Buttered Rum Is Irresistible." The Spruce Eats. The Spruce Eats. August 30. https://www.thespruceeats.com/hot-buttered-rum-recipe-759309.

"Christmas: 36-Hour Seafood Marathon." 2023. Christmas | 36-Hour Seafood Marathon. Accessed October 1. https://www.sydneyfishmarket.com.au/Christmas.

Bendfeldt-Diaz, Paula. 2023. "The Best Guatemalan Tamal Colorado Recipe." Growing Up Bilingual. March 12. https://growingupbilingual.com/the-best-recipe-for-guatemalan-tamales-colorados/.

TIEMPO, Tendencias EL. 2020. "Aprenda a Hacer, Fácil y Rápido, Natilla y Buñuelos Para Las Novenas." El Tiempo. El Tiempo. December 21. https://www.eltiempo.com/cultura/gastronomia/receta-bunuelos-y-natilla-como-preparar-natilla-colombiana-y-bunuelos-navidad-y-novena-555757.

"TABLA DE CORTE, QUESO EL VISO Y ACCESORIO." 2023. Buy Our Natural Cider. Accessed October 1. https://www.productosdeasturias.com/en/asturias-cider.

"Largest Gingerbread Man." 2023. Guinness World Records. Accessed October 1. https://www.guinnessworldrecords.com/world-records/largest-gingerbread-man.

Reynolds, John. 2023. "Christmas Dinner in Brazil." Texas de Brazil. Accessed October 1. https://texasdebrazil.com/churrasco-recipes/christmas-dinner-in-brazil.

"Julmust." 2023. Wikipedia. Wikimedia Foundation. July 9. https://en.wikipedia.org/wiki/Julmust.

The Economics of Christmas

Beneath the shimmering lights, jubilant carols, and heartwarming traditions, Christmas holds its own in the vast arena of global economics. It's a season that significantly impacts industries, employment rates, and market trends. From the sprightly elves in the workshops of small artisans to the bustling activity in the world's largest factories, the yuletide season drives a financial momentum like no other.

As we unwrap the fiscal facets of this festive period, prepare to delve into the intricate dance of supply and demand, understand the spending patterns of households, and appreciate the immense economic machinery powered by Christmas cheer.

In 2019, U.S. holiday retail sales reached around $730.2 billion. That's more than the GDP of some countries!

🎁 🎁 🎁

Black Friday, which kicks off the Christmas shopping season, saw 93.2 million online buyers in 2019. That's like the entire population of Germany going mouse-click crazy!

🎁 🎁 🎁

Evergreen Christmas trees have been sold commercially in the United States since 1850. They're the original "going green" for Christmas.

In the UK, an estimated £700 million is spent on unwanted Christmas gifts each year, with £42 million's worth ending up in landfill each year. It's the season of giving... and apparently, discarding!

🎁 🎁 🎁

In 2020, Amazon shipped a record-breaking 1.5 billion packages during the festive season. Reindeers are now considering a career change!

🎁 🎁 🎁

More than 1.3 billion Christmas cards are purchased each year in the U.S. That's a lot of Hallmark moments.

🎁 🎁 🎁

An estimated 25-30 million real Christmas trees are sold in the United States each year. Douglas firs are striking it rich!

LEGO, the popular toy company, makes more than 60 billion bricks each year. That's enough to build Santa a holiday home.

🎁 🎁 🎁

The average American drops a week's worth of wages on Christmas gifts each year. That's a serious sleigh-load of generosity!

🎁 🎁 🎁

In 2020, it was estimated that each American would spend an average of $998 on gifts, food, and decorations. Ho, ho, whoa!

While 51% of U.S. shoppers get a jumpstart on Christmas shopping before November, their neighbors in Canada play it cool with just 36% starting early. Meanwhile, Singles Day in China kicks off the festive frenzy in early November. But Brazilians? Only 13% are catching the October Christmas spirit!

🎁 🎁 🎁

The town of Yiwu in China is known as "Christmas village" as it produces an estimated 80% of the world's Christmas trinkets and decorations. Santa might have some outsourcing secrets!

🎁 🎁 🎁

The waste generated each year from gift wrap and shopping bags totals over 4 million tons in the U.S. alone. That could wrap the Earth how many times?!

In Australia, $400 million is expected to be spent on a collective 35 million individual gifts that nobody wants. It's the thought that costs!

🎁 🎁 🎁

The Rockefeller Center Christmas Tree in New York City is more than just a festive display—it's an economic boon for the city. Over three times as many tourists visit the famous building during the festive period.

🎁 🎁 🎁

U.S. retailers are set to hire only 410,000 seasonal workers in 2023, the lowest since the 2008 recession. That's a 26% drop from 2022! Tight budgets and economic concerns are giving Santa a staffing challenge.

In 2020, e-commerce saw a 32.2% increase in holiday sales compared to the previous year. Click, click, ho!

🎁 🎁 🎁

The cost of all the gifts in the "Twelve Days of Christmas" song was estimated to be $45,523.27 in 2022, a 10% increase on the year before. Who knew true love was so pricey?

🎁 🎁 🎁

Around 40% of the year's battery sales occur in the festive period. It's the most electric time of the year!

🎁 🎁 🎁

Christmas accounts for 19% of all retail sales in the United States. Santa Claus is coming to Wall Street!

The popular Christmas flower, poinsettia, brings in about $250 million to the U.S. economy. That's a lot of flower power!

🎁 🎁 🎁

In Germany, the most popular Christmas gift is books. Paging through the holiday spirit!

🎁 🎁 🎁

Due to increased holiday shopping in 2022, around 36% of shoppers went into debt over Christmas. Deck the halls with bills and statements!

🎁 🎁 🎁

In a 2022 survey, 78% of consumers said they purchased a gift card for Christmas. It's the one size fits all of holiday gifting!

The global Christmas decorations market was valued at $5.52 billion in 2021. Sparkle and shine have a price tag!

🎁 🎁 🎁

Approximately 12,000 people are treated in emergency rooms each year due to holiday decorating mishaps in the U.S. Yule be sorry!

🎁 🎁 🎁

In 2012, the "Home Alone" house was sold for $1.585 million, a significant drop from its original asking price of $2.4 million. It seems even iconic movie homes aren't immune to the real estate market's ebbs and flows!

🎁 🎁 🎁

In Finland, a Christmas peace declaration has been read in Turku every year since the 1300s, except during times of war. Peace on Earth isn't priceless!

According to the USPS, December 14 is their busiest day in the office, with just 11 days to Christmas! But hold onto your stockings, because December 21 sees the real sleigh action with over 30 million packages landing on doorsteps.

🎁 🎁 🎁

Each year in the U.S., fire departments tackle around 210 Christmas tree fires, leading to an average of 6 fatalities, 16 injuries, and a blazing $16.2 million in property damage. Tree safety isn't just tinsel talk!

🎁 🎁 🎁

Christmas bulbs may be tiny, but they're power-hungry! The U.S. uses enough holiday light energy annually to power 14 million fridges. Talk about a bright appetite! Eco-friendly Rudolph, where are you?

A 2022 survey found that 85% of people prefer to shop for Christmas gifts online to avoid crowds. Cyber sleigh all the way!

🎁 🎁 🎁

In the Netherlands, Sinterklaas gives out "chocolate letters," representing a person's first initial. That's some edible education!

🎁 🎁 🎁

Fruitcake can remain edible for many years.
In 2017, a 106-year-old fruitcake was found in Antarctica, still "almost" edible. The gift that keeps on not giving!

🎁 🎁 🎁

In the UK, the Christmas retail market is worth an estimated £82 billion. That's enough to buy the North Pole and turn it into a theme park!

The U.S. confectionery industry makes about $1.4 billion during the winter holiday season. Talk about a sugar high!

🎁 🎁 🎁

Mariah Carey's "All I Want for Christmas Is You" has earned over $60 million in royalties since its release in 1994. She's the real Queen of the North!

🎁 🎁 🎁

The estimated market value of the U.S. toy industry was $32.6 billion in 2020, and a significant chunk of that comes from Christmas toy sales. Santa's going to need a bigger bag!

🎁 🎁 🎁

A study revealed that Americans spend an average of 15 hours shopping for Christmas gifts. That's almost two full workdays!

Household waste in the U.S. increases by 25% between Thanksgiving and New Year's Day. A stark reminder to be mindful during the festive season!

🎁 🎁 🎁

Cyber Monday sales in 2022 reached $11.3 billion, making it the largest online shopping day in U.S. history up to that point.

🎁 🎁 🎁

Small Business Saturday, which encourages consumers to visit brick and mortar businesses, founded by American Express in 2010, saw U.S. consumers spend an estimated $17.9 billion at independent retailers and restaurants in 2022. Shop local, support global!

In 2022, 166.3 million U.S. consumers shopped from Thanksgiving Day through Cyber Monday. That's more people than watched the Super Bowl!

🎁 🎁 🎁

Americans splurge an average of $50 on Christmas gifts for their pets! With 34% gifting their dogs and 22% their cats, it seems our furry friends are out-pacing in-laws, who only receive gifts from 19%. Woof, that's some pet preference!

🎁 🎁 🎁

By 2029, the global market for artificial Christmas trees is set to hit $3.14 billion. North America's taking the lead, aiming for $1.64 billion. Guess real trees are so last millennium!

Christmas Day sees a spike in mobile app downloads, as people get new phones and tablets as gifts. There's an app for that holiday cheer!

🎁 🎁 🎁

The average Christmas tree contains about 25,000 bugs and insects. It's a jolly jungle in there!

🎁 🎁 🎁

The busiest shopping day of the year isn't Black Friday; it's actually the Saturday before Christmas, often called "Super Saturday." Santa's sleigh has nothing on these last-minute shoppers!

🎁 🎁 🎁

According to a recent survey, 33% of Americans would rather skip the holidays to avoid gift expenses. Why? A whopping 46% are in credit card debt, and over half struggle with holiday budgets.

The U.S. airline industry carries around 50 million passengers during the 18-day winter holiday travel period. Who needs a sleigh when you have a jet?

🎁 🎁 🎁

Hallmark introduced its first Christmas cards in 1915, five years after the founding of the company. It was the original "DM slide" for holiday wishes!

🎁 🎁 🎁

The total commercial value of Christmas is estimated at over $900 billion in the United States. Makes those five golden rings seem like pocket change!

The North American Aerospace Defense Command (NORAD) has been tracking Santa Claus on Christmas Eve since 1955. It started when a child accidentally dialed the unlisted phone number of the Director of Operations at NORAD. Best misdial ever!

🎁 🎁 🎁

Wrapping paper sales in the United States are estimated at $2.6 billion yearly. That's literally money you're ripping apart!

🎁 🎁 🎁

Surveys reveal that 61% of Americans received an unwanted gift at Christmas. The least-desirable gifts are clothing and accessories (43%). It's the thought that counts, even if it's recycled!

For immediate release January 16, and NRF President and CEO Matthew Shay. 2020. "NRF Says 2019 Holiday Sales Were up 4.1 Percent." NRF. https://nrf.com/media-center/press-releases/nrf-says-2019-holiday-sales-were-41-percent.

"Cyber Black Friday." 2022. Wikipedia. Wikimedia Foundation. November 25. https://en.wikipedia.org/wiki/Cyber_Black_Friday.

Dixie Sandborn, Michigan State University Extension. 2022. "Real Christmas Trees: History, Facts and Environmental Impacts." MSU Extension. https://www.canr.msu.edu/news/real_christmas_trees_history_facts_and_environmental_impacts.

"What to Do with Unwanted Christmas Gifts." 2023. WeBuyBooks. Accessed October 1. https://www.webuybooks.co.uk/blog/what-to-do-with-unwanted-christmas-gifts/.

Mlot, Stephanie. 2020. "Amazon Delivers 1.5 Billion Packages During 'Record-Breaking' Holiday Season." PCMAG. PCMag. December 30. https://www.pcmag.com/news/amazon-delivers-15-billion-packages-during-record-breaking-holiday-season.

"Christmas Cards." 2023. Hallmark Corporate. https://corporate.hallmark.com/hallmark-news/christmas-cards.

"Quick Tree Facts: National Christmas Tree Association." 2019. National Christmas Tree Association | Every Christmas Needs a Real Tree. July 29. https://realchristmastrees.org/education/quick-tree-facts.

Thaler, Shannon. 2023. "Lego Abandons Efforts to Make Bricks from Recycled Plastic Bottles after Finding It Didn't Reduce CO2 Emissions." New York Post. New York Post. September 25. https://nypost.com/2023/09/25/lego-ditches-effort-to-make-bricks-from-recycled-bottles/.

Howarth, Josh. 2022. "How Much Do Americans Spend On Christmas? (Latest Data)." Exploding Topics. Exploding Topics. August 6. https://exploding-topics.com/blog/christmas-spending-stats.

"Holiday Trends Blog 3." 2023. Sensormatic. Accessed October 1. https://www.sensormatic.com/en_ca/resources/ar/2021/holiday-trends-blog-3.

Roman Kierst (小). 2023. "These Christmas Factories in China Churn Out Most of the World's Holiday Decorations." The World of Chinese. Accessed October 1. https://www.theworldofchinese.com/2022/12/behind-the-scenes-at-chinas-christmas-factories/.

"User." All Things Supply Chain - Supply Chain Trends, Best Practices, News and Much More! December 14. https://www.allthingssupplychain.com/the-wrapping-paper-waste-problem-and-what-can-be-done-about-it/.

Duffy, Emma. 2019. "Aussies Wasted over $400 Million in Unwanted Christmas Gifts Last Year." Savings.Com.Au. November 18. https://www.savings.com.au/news/aussies-wasted-over-400-million-in-unwanted-christmas-gifts-last-year.

Slotnik, Daniel E. 2020. "How to See the Rockefeller Center Christmas Tree." The New York Times. The New York Times. December 2. https://www.nytimes.com/2020/12/02/nyregion/rockefeller-tree-lighting.html.

Cavale, Siddharth. 2023. "Exclusive: US Retailer Holiday Hiring to Drop to Levels Last Seen in 2008." Reuters. Thomson Reuters. September 15. https://www.reuters.com/markets/us/us-retailer-holiday-hiring-drop-levels-last-seen-2018-report-2023-09-15/.

Laurenthomas. 2021. "Americans Spent a Record Online over 2020 Holidays, and More e-Commerce Gains Are Expected." CNBC. CNBC. https://www.cnbc.com/2021/01/12/holiday-2020-spending-online-surges-32percent-to-188point2-billion-adobe.html.

Aldinger, Carl. 2022. "How Much the '12 Days of Christmas' Will Cost You with 2022's Inflation." WETM - MyTwinTiers.Com. WETM - MyTwinTiers.com. December 15. https://www.mytwintiers.com/news-header/economy/what-the-12-days-of-christmas-will-cost-you-with-2022s-inflation.

"My Light Shines on in the Darkness Battery Sales Shine over Christmas and in the Winter Months: Grocery Trader." 2020. Grocery Trader | Grocer News from Grocery Trader - Latest News and Information for the Multiple Grocery Trade in the UK. June 11. https://grocerytrader.co.uk/my-light-shines-on-in-the-darkness-battery-sales-shine-over-christmas-and-in-the-winter-months/.

"Winter FAQs." 2023. NRF. Accessed October 1. https://nrf.com/research-insights/holiday-data-and-trends/winter-holidays/winter-holiday-faqs.

"Poinsettia." 2023. Wikipedia. Wikimedia Foundation. August 17. https://en.wikipedia.org/wiki/Poinsettia.

Süßmann, Ingrid. 2016. "Books Top Holiday Gift-Giving Lists in Germany." Publishing Perspectives. November 30. https://publishingperspectives.com/2016/12/books-top-holiday-gift-giving-lists-germany.

Jdickler. 2022. "1 in 3 Americans Overspent during the Holidays, Boosting Credit Card Balances." CNBC. CNBC. https://www.cnbc.com/2022/01/06/americans-overspent-during-the-holidays-increasing-credit-card-debt.html.

"Results from the 2022 Holiday Gift Card Study." 2023. GiftCardGranny.Com. Accessed October 1. https://www.giftcardgranny.com/blog/2022-gift-card-trends/.

"Global Christmas Decoration Market Size, Share & Growth Analysis Report, 2022-2030." 2023. Polaris. Accessed October 1. https://www.polaris-marketresearch.com/industry-analysis/christmas-decoration-market.

"'Deck the Halls' Safely" 2023. U.S. Consumer Product Safety Commission. Accessed October 1. https://www.cpsc.gov/Newsroom/News-Releases/2014/CPSC-Estimates-More-Than-15000-Holiday-Decorating-Injuries-During-November-and-December.

The Hill. 2018. "58 Percent of Americans Prefer Online Shopping to In-Store Purchases during Holiday Season." The Hill. The Hill. December 7. https://thehill.com/hilltv/what-americas-thinking/420272-41-percent-say-they-prefer-shopping-in-stores-during-the/.

"The Declaration of Christmas Peace in Turku." 2023. Wiki. Accessed October 1. https://wiki.aineetonkulttuuriperinto.fi/wiki/The_Declaration_of_Christmas_Peace_in_Turku.

"Here's How Much The Iconic Home Alone House Is Worth Today." 2022. K 104.7. November 29. https://k1047.com/2022/11/29/heres-how-much-the-iconic-home-alone-house-is-worth-today/.

"Christmas Card Statistics." 2017. Alexanders Print Advantage - Web To Print Experts. December 18. https://alexanders.com/blog/christmas-card-statistics/.

"Holiday Fire Safety." 2022. NIST. December 13. https://www.nist.gov/fire/holiday-fire-safety.

"How Much Electricity Do Christmas Lights Use?" 2023. Mr. Electric. Accessed October 1. https://mrelectric.com/blog/how-much-electricity-do-christmas-lights-use.

Thayer, Travis. 2023. "Survey: One-Third of Americans Have Already Started Their Holiday Shopping." Eagle Country 99.3. Eagle Country 99.3. September 12. https://www.eaglecountryonline.com/news/local-news/survey-one-third-of-americans-have-already-started-their-holiday-shopping.

Smith, P. 2023. "Topic: UK Christmas Shopping." Statista. Accessed October 1. https://www.statista.com/topics/3157/uk-christmas-shopping/#topicOverview.

"Candy Cane." 2023. How Products Are Made. Accessed October 1. http://www.madehow.com/Volume-7/Candy-Cane.html.

Gittins, William. 2022. "How Much Money...?" Diario AS. December 17. https://en.as.com/latest_news/how-much-money-does-mariah-carey-make-every-year-thanks-to-all-i-want-for-christmas-is-you-n.

Guangdong Jialang Industry Co., Ltd. 2023. "Annual U.S. Toy Industry for 2020 Sales Data." LinkedIn. Accessed October 1. https://www.linkedin.com/pulse/annual-us-toy-industry-2020-sales-data-btop.

Zagorsky, Jay L. 2019. "How Much You Should Spend on Holiday Gifts, According to an Economist." PBS. Public Broadcasting Service. November 28. https://www.pbs.org/newshour/economy/making-sense/how-much-you-should-spend-on-holiday-gifts-according-to-an-economist.

Nolte, Catherine. 2021. "The Pandemic Creates the Perfect Storm for Food Waste during the Holidays." Southwest Times Record. Fort Smith Times Record. December 15. https://eu.swtimes.com/story/news/2021/12/15/food-waste-during-holidays-impacts-more-than-just-your-wallet/6423511001/.

Shewale, Rohit. 2023. "52 Cyber Monday Statistics 2023 (Discounts, Sales & Trends)." DemandSage. September 11. https://www.demandsage.com/cyber-monday-statistics/.

"Small Business Saturday." 2023. U.S. Small Business Administration. Accessed October 1. https://www.sba.gov/about-sba/organization/sba-initiatives/small-business-saturday.

Devarakonda, Mythili. 2022. "Almost 200 Million People Shopped during This Year's Thanksgiving Weekend." CNS Maryland. CNS Maryland. December 8. https://cnsmaryland.org/2022/12/07/almost-200-million-people-shopped-during-this-years-thanksgiving-weekend/.

Sneha Mali, Cognitive Market Research. 2023. "Artificial Christmas Trees Market Size Will Be $3,146.02 Million by 2029!" Cognitive Market Research. September 20. https://www.cognitivemarketresearch.com/artificial-christmas-trees-market-report.

Wharton Women. 2023. "How Much Do Americans Really Spend on Christmas? And What Is Everyone Buying?" Wharton Women. Wharton Women. February 17. http://www.whartonwomen-penn.com/walnutstreetjournal/christmasspending.

"How Mobile Apps Performed during the 2022 Holidays." 2023. Adjust. Accessed October 1. https://www.adjust.com/blog/mobile-app-trends-over-the-holidays-2022-installs-and-sessions/.

Kirkpatrick, Noel. 2021. "There Are Up to 25,000 Bugs in the Average Christmas Tree." Treehugger. Treehugger. November 8. https://www.treehugger.com/bugs-christmas-tree-4862443.

Moore, Logan. 2021. "Busiest Shopping Day of the Holidays Is Here." Barrons. Barrons. December 18. https://www.barrons.com/articles/super-saturday-busiest-shopping-day-holiday-season-51639781932.

Ashford, Kate. 2017. "A Third Of Americans Would Rather Skip The Holidays." Forbes. Forbes Magazine. November 30. https://www.forbes.com/sites/kateashford/2017/11/29/skip-holidays/.

Wichter, Zach. 2022. "Keep an Eye on Your Christmas Flight: Here's What Flyers Should Expect This Week." USA Today. Gannett Satellite Information Network. December 21. https://eu.usatoday.com/story/travel/airline-news/2022/12/20/busiest-day-time-holiday-flights/10927600002/.

Magazine, Smithsonian. 2015. "The History of the Christmas Card." Smithsonian.Com. Smithsonian Institution. December 9. https://www.smithsonianmag.com/history/history-christmas-card-180957487/.

"NORAD Tracks Santa." 2023. Wikipedia. Wikimedia Foundation. September 27. https://en.wikipedia.org/wiki/NORAD_Tracks_Santa.

Sabanoglu, Tugba. 2023. "Holiday Retail Sales in the United States 2002-2022." Statista. August 30. https://www.statista.com/statistics/243439/holiday-retail-sales-in-the-united-states.

"How Much Should You Really Spend on Wrapping Paper?" 2023. Yahoo! Finance. Yahoo! Accessed October 1. https://finance.yahoo.com/news/much-really-spend-wrapping-paper-213818742.html.

Quirky Christmas Facts

Ah, Christmas! A time of tradition, warmth, and... peculiarity? Indeed, beyond the familiar jingles and time-honored tales, Christmas is brimming with oddities and unexpected tales. From bizarre traditions tucked away in the nooks and crannies of the world to surprising historical tidbits about our most beloved holiday elements, this chapter invites you on a whimsical sleigh ride through the more unconventional side of the festive season. Ready your reindeer and tighten your Santa hat, because we're about to dive deep into a snowdrift of delightful Christmas eccentricities!

Every winter at Switzerland's Samnaun Ski Resort, Santa enthusiasts compete in "ClauWau," the Santa World Championships. Teams of Santas race on snowmobiles, climb chimneys, and ski down slopes— all to be crowned the ultimate Santa Claus World Champions. Winter Olympics, eat your heart out!

✳ ✳ ✳

The town of Gävle, Sweden, erects a giant straw goat every Christmas. More often than not, it gets burned down in a massive Yule-tide blaze. Some people just want to watch the world (or at least the goat) burn!

✳ ✳ ✳

In the early 20th century, Christmas Eve was less about jingling bells and more about chilling tales. Folks would gather around to share ghost stories, making it the spookiest night before a festive day. Forget decking the halls; they were busy checking under the bed!

In 2001, the astronauts aboard the International Space Station celebrated Christmas with vacuum-packed turkey. Space stuffing, anyone?

✳ ✳ ✳

The world record for the most lights on a Christmas tree was set in Belgium in 2010 with 194,672 lights. Take that, Clark Griswold!

✳ ✳ ✳

In 2019, the city of San Jose del Monte in Bulacan, Philippines, set the record for the world's largest "Living Nativity Scene" with a whopping 2,101 participants. That's what you call a truly massive manger crowd!

In some parts of Catholic Germany, it's considered unlucky to take down the Christmas tree before February 2nd, Candlemas. So, if you thought you were late in packing away the holiday decor, think again!

✳ ✳ ✳

The world's largest snow maze was created in Canada in 2019 and measured 2,789 square meters. It's all fun and games until you can't find your way out!

✳ ✳ ✳

In Greek folklore, mischievous goblins called Kalikantzari are said to cause chaos during the 12 days of Christmas. Beware of these mythical holiday pranksters!

The risk of heart attack is highest on Christmas Eve, specifically around 10 p.m. It's not the ghost of Christmas future you should be afraid of, it's the gravy!

* * *

In South Korea, Christmas is often treated like Valentine's Day— a romantic holiday for couples to exchange gifts and go on dates. Mistletoe for two, please!

* * *

The tradition of writing letters to Santa Claus is believed to have started in the U.S. in the 19th century, but these days, the big guy gets emails too. Even Santa can't escape spam!

According to an old British superstition, each mince pie eaten during the 12 Days of Christmas will bring a month of happiness in the coming year. Talk about pie in the sky!

In 2013, Shanghai set a Guinness World Record for the longest Christmas cake ever, measuring a whopping 1,068 meters (3,504 feet). Crafted by 80 chefs from the Pudong Shangri-la Hotel, it took days of preparation, 150 staff members, and 24 hours of continuous work. This vanilla-flavored log with bitter chocolate frosting wasn't just for show—it raised funds for children with cancer. Now that's a sweet achievement!

Did you know that Santa has an official North Pole mailing address? Children can mail their letters to "Santa Claus, North Pole, H0H 0H0, Canada." Those Canadian postal workers must be elves in disguise!

✳ ✳ ✳

Feeling frosty? Bethel, Maine, in the United States holds the world record for the tallest snowman , named "Olympia." In 2008, Olympia reached a height of 122 feet and 1 inch!

✳ ✳ ✳

A small town in Indiana, USA, is named "Santa Claus." Unsurprisingly, it receives thousands of letters addressed to the jolly old elf every December.

A popular Christmas tradition in Venezuela's capital, Caracas, is for the streets to be closed off on Christmas Eve so that people can roller-skate to church!

＊＊＊

The state of Oklahoma in the USA didn't declare Christmas a legal holiday until 1907. Talk about late to the party!

＊＊＊

The Canary Islands have a unique way of celebrating: instead of snowmen, they build sandmen on their beautiful beaches.

Approximately 70% of toys worldwide are manufactured in China. So, chances are, a toy from Santa's sleigh has a "Made in China" tag.

* * *

In the past, the song 'We Wish You a Merry Christmas' was less of a jolly carol and more of a festive threat. So, next time you sing, 'Bring us some figgy pudding!' remember – they weren't asking, they were demanding! Yuletide yikes!

* * *

Ever wondered why we exchange gifts during Christmas? While Christians believe it's to mirror the Three Wise Men's offerings, it turns out pagans were also sliding into the gifting scene with offerings to their gods. So, whether it's for Jesus or Jupiter, the tradition stands strong. Double the reason, double the presents!

Decking the halls with evergreens? Thank the ancient Egyptians and Romans for that! They used them during winter solstice as a stylish reminder that spring's greenery was just a calendar flip away. So, next time you're tinseling that tree, remember, it's a millennia-old reminder that warmer days are coming!

* * *

Thinking of Dasher and Dancer? Well, they almost had coworkers named Flossie and Glossie! Before settling on the famous reindeer names we know, options like Racer, Pacer, and even... Feckless were on the table.

* * *

With around 85% of Americans celebrating the holiday, it's no wonder stores deck the halls ASAP. And while not everyone dives deep into the religious side of things, most are certainly unwrapping joy (and gifts!) come December 25.

Christmas church attendance: it's not just about festive hymns, it's a bipartisan affair! While 65% of Republicans are gearing up to celebrate with a sermon, 45% of Democrats are planning to jingle all the way... to the pew. Politics aside, Christmas spirit unites!

**

The Rockefeller Christmas Tree had humble beginnings — think Charlie Brown vibes in 1931. From a tiny tree on a construction site to today's dazzling 25,000-light spectacle, it's the ultimate holiday 'glow-up.' Selfie, anyone?

**

The world's largest floating Christmas tree, as of 2014, is in Rio de Janeiro and measures 278 feet in height. Talk about going overboard—literally.

Sources

Farnsworth, Audrey. 2018. "Santas Are Gathering in Switzerland in Hopes of Becoming World Champions and 5 Other Santa-Related Events." Fodors Travel Guide. Fodors Travel Guide. November 15. https://www.fodors.com/news/trip-ideas/santas-are-gathering-in-switzerland-in-hopes-of-becoming-world-champions-and-5-other-santa-related-events.

"Gävle Goat." 2023. Wikipedia. Wikimedia Foundation. September 27. https://en.wikipedia.org/wiki/G%C3%A4vle_goat.

"How Ghost Stories Became a Christmas Tradition in Victorian England." 2023. History.Com. A&E Television Networks. Accessed October 1. https://www.history.com/news/christmas-tradition-ghost-stories.

"Thanksgiving Day in Space." 2023. Homepage. Accessed October 1. https://airandspace.si.edu/stories/editorial/thanksgiving-day-space.

"Most Living Figures in a Nativity Scene." 2023. Guinness World Records. Accessed October 1. https://www.guinnessworldrecords.com/world-records/most-living-figures-in-a-nativity-scene.

Karenanne. 2022. "When Do You Take Down the Christmas Tree?" A German Girl in America. December 26. https://germangirlinamerica.com/take-down-christmas-tree/.

"Largest Snow Maze." 2023. Guinness World Records. Accessed October 1. https://www.guinnessworldrecords.com/world-records/114366-largest-maze-snow-maze.

Liacopoulou, Ivy. 2020. "Kalikantzari and Theophaneia." Kopiaste..to Greek Hospitality. https://www.kopiaste.org/2009/01/kalikantzari-and-theo-phaneia/.

2023. ABC News. ABC News Network. Accessed October 1. https://abc-news.go.com/Health/risk-heart-attack-peaks-christmas-eve-study/story?id=59999262.

"Black Day (South Korea)." 2023. Wikipedia. Wikimedia Foundation. September 28. https://en.wikipedia.org/wiki/Black_Day_(South_Korea).

Magazine, Smithsonian. 2015. "A Brief History of Sending a Letter to Santa." Smithsonian.Com. Smithsonian Institution. December 3. https://www.smith-sonianmag.com/arts-culture/brief-history-sending-letter-santa-180957441.

Speakeasy. 2021. "Quirky Christmas Traditions in the UK - SpeakEasy - School of English." SpeakEasy. September 21. https://www.speakeasyschool.co.uk/quirky-christmas-traditions-in-the-uk.

Press, Associated. 2011. "China Sets the Record for World's Longest Christmas Cake." NDTV.Com. December 1. https://www.ndtv.com/world-news/china-sets-the-record-for-worlds-longest-christmas-cake-570307.

Post, Canada. 2023. "Santa Letter Program: Our Company." Santa Letter Program | Our Company | Canada Post. Accessed October 1. https://www.canadapost-postescanada.ca/cpc/en/our-company/giving-back-to-our-communities/write-a-letter-to-santa.page.

Emily Burnham, Bangor Daily News. 2023. "Maine Still Holds the World Record for the Tallest Snowman." WPFO. Accessed October 1. https://fox23maine.com/news/local/maine-still-holds-the-world-record-for-the-tallest-snowman-snow-people-guinness-world-records-bethel-climate-change-angus-king-of-the-mountain-olympia-snowwoman.

"Santa Claus, Indiana." 2023. Wikipedia. Wikimedia Foundation. August 27. https://en.wikipedia.org/wiki/Santa_Claus,_Indiana.

Trending, FP. 2020. "From Hiding Brooms in Norway to Venezuela's Roller Blades, Some Peculiar Christmas Traditions around the World-World News, Firstpost." Firstpost. Firstpost. December 24. https://www.firstpost.com/world/from-hiding-brooms-in-norway-to-venezuelas-roller-blades-some-peculiar-christmas-traditions-around-the-world-9142861.html.

Editors, Southern Living. 2023. "This Southern State Was the First to Make Christmas a Legal Holiday." Southern Living. Southern Living. March 5. https://www.southernliving.com/travel/christmas-south-southern-city-legal-holiday.

eMascaró. 2022. "3 Reasons to Visit the Canary Islands in Winter - HD Hotels." Hoteles En Canarias - HD Hotels. June 6. https://www.hdhotels.com/en/blog/canary-islands-in-winter/.

2023. HKTDC Research. Accessed October 1. https://research.hktdc.com/en/article/MzA3ODUwOTUx.

Ruehl, Kim. 2018. "Folk Song History of We Wish You a Merry Christmas." LiveAbout. LiveAbout. https://www.liveabout.com/we-wish-you-a-merry-christmas-1322366.

Staff, The Week. 2014. "A Brief History of the Christmas Present." Theweek. The Week. December 20. https://theweek.com/articles/441360/brief-history-christmas-present.

"History of Christmas Trees - Symbolism, Traditions & Trivia." 2023. History. Com. A&E Television Networks. Accessed October 1. https://www.history.com/topics/christmas/history-of-christmas-trees.

Hollandbeck, Andy. 2019. "In a Word: Eight, Er, Nine Tiny Reindeer." The Saturday Evening Post. December 18. https://www.saturdayeveningpost.com/2019/12/in-a-word-eight-er-nine-tiny-reindeer/.

Statista. 2023. "Topic: National Holidays in the United States." Statista. Accessed October 1. https://www.statista.com/topics/3216/national-holidays-in-the-us/#topicOverview.

Author, No. 2017. "Americans Say Religious Aspects of Christmas Are Declining in Public Life." Pew Research Center's Religion & Public Life Project.

Pew Research Center. December 12. https://www.pewresearch.org/religion/2017/12/12/americans-say-religious-aspects-of-christmas-are-declining-in-public-life/.

Adams, Scott. 2022. "The History of Rio's Floating Christmas Tree - A Connect Brazil Video List." Connect Brazil. March 31. https://www.connectbrazil.com/the-history-of-rios-floating-christmas-tree/.

And there you have it, under the mistletoe and twinkling lights! May these festive facts sprinkle your conversations with holiday magic and joy.

If this book added a jingle to your step, I'd be ever so grateful for a **review**. Each one is like a gift under the tree, guiding me to craft even merrier books next time!

Craving more fabulous facts?
Jingle on over to:
www.bellanovabooks.com

Still feeling festive?!

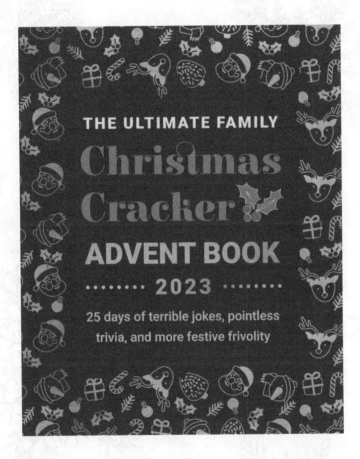

**Festive fun for the whole family!
Available NOW in all major
online bookstores .**